The Spanish Gypsy...

George Eliot

E SPANISH GYPSY

BY

GEORGE ELIOT

NEW YORK
WHITE, STOKES, AND ALLEN
1886

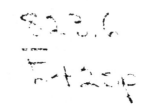

This work was originally written in the winter of 1864–65; after a visit to Spain in 1867 it was rewritten and amplified. The reader conversant with Spanish poetry will see that in two of the Lyrics an attempt has been made to imitate the trochaic measure and assonance of the Spanish Ballad.

trochee (tro-kee)
two syllables – a long followed by a short, or
a stressed followed by an unstressed in accentual meter.
(1st syllable stressed).

Iambic – 2nd syllable stressed

THE SPANISH GYPSY.

BOOK I.

'TIS the warm South, where Europe spreads her
    lands
Like fretted leaflets, breathing on the deep:
Broad-breasted Spain, leaning with equal love
On the Mid Sea that moans with memories,
And on the untravelled Ocean's restless tides.
This river, shadowed by the battlements
And gleaming silvery toward the northern sky,
Feeds the famed stream that waters Andalus
And loiters, amorous of the fragrant air,
By Córdova and Seville to the bay
Fronting Algarva and the wandering flood
Of Guadiana.   This deep mountain gorge
Slopes widening on the olive-pluméd plains
Of fair Granáda : one far-stretching arm
Points to Elvira, one to eastward heights
Of Alpujarras where the new-bathed Day
With oriflamme uplifted o'er the peaks
Saddens the breasts of northward-looking snows
That loved the night, and soared with soaring
    stars ;
Flashing the signals of his nearing swiftness
From Almería's purple-shadowed bay
On to the far-off rocks that gaze and glow—
On to Alhambra, strong and ruddy heart

Of glorious Morisma, gasping now,
A maiméd giant in his agony.
This town that dips its feet within the stream,
And seems to sit a tower-crowned Cybele,
Spreading her ample robe adown the rocks,
Is rich Bedmár : 'twas Moorish long ago,
But now the Cross is sparkling on the Mosque,
And bells make Catholic the trembling air.
The fortress gleams in Spanish sunshine now
('Tis south a mile before the rays are Moorish)—
Hereditary jewel, agraffe bright
On all the many-titled privilege
Of young Duke Silva.   No Castilian knight
That serves Queen Isabel has higher charge ;
For near this frontier sits the Moorish king,
Not Boabdil the waverer, who usurps
A throne he trembles in, and fawning licks
The feet of conquerors, but that fierce lion
Grisly El Zagal, who has made his lair
In Guadix' fort, and rushing thence with strength,
Half his own fierceness, half the untainted heart
Of mountain bands that fight for holiday,
Wastes the fair lands that lie by Alcalá,
Wreathing his horse's neck with Christian heads.

To keep the Christian frontier—such high trust
Is young Duke Silva's ; and the time is great.
(What times are little ?   To the sentinel
That hour is regal when he mounts on guard.)
The fifteenth century since the Man Divine
Taught and was hated in Capernaum
Is near its end—is falling as a husk
Away from all the fruit its years have riped.
The Moslem faith, now flickering like a torch
In a night struggle on this shore of Spain,
Glares, a broad column of advancing flame,
Along the Danube and the Illyrian shore

Far into Italy, where eager monks,
Who watch in dreams and dream the while they
      watch,
See Christ grow paler in the baleful light,
Crying again the cry of the forsaken.
But faith, the stronger for extremity,
Becomes prophetic, hears the far-off tread
Of western chivalry, sees downward sweep
The archangel Michael with the gleaming sword,
And listens for the shriek of hurrying fiends
Chased from their revels in God's sanctuary.
So trusts the monk, and lifts appealing eyes
To the high dome, the Church's firmament,
Where the blue light-pierced curtain, rolled away,
Reveals the throne and Him who sits thereon.
So trust the men whose best hope for the world
Is ever that the world is near its end :
Impatient of the stars that keep their course
And make no pathway for the coming Judge.

But other futures stir the world's great heart.
The West now enters on the heritage
Won from the tombs of mighty ancestors,
The seeds, the gold, the gems, the silent harps
That lay deep buried with the memories
Of old renown.
No more, as once in sunny Avignon,
The poet-scholar spreads the Homeric page,
And gazes sadly, like the deaf at song ;
For now the old epic voices ring again
And vibrate with the beat and melody
Stirred by the warmth of old Ionian days.
The martyred sage, the Attic orator,
Immortally incarnate, like the gods,
In spiritual bodies, wingèd words
Holding a universe impalpable,
Find a new audience.   For evermore,

With grander resurrection than was feigned
Of Attila's fierce Huns, the soul of Greece
Conquers the bulk of Persia.   The maimed form
Of calmly-joyous beauty, marble-limbed,
Yet breathing with the thought that shaped its
      lips,
Looks mild reproach from out its opened grave
At creeds of terror ; and the vine-wreathed god
Fronts the pierced Image with the crown of
      thorns.
The soul of man is widening toward the past :
No longer hanging at the breast of life
Feeding in blindness to his parentage—
Quenching all wonder with Omnipotence,
Praising a name with indolent piety—
He spells the record of his long descent,
More largely conscious of the life that was.
And from the height that shows where morning
      shone
On far-off summits pale and gloomy now,
The horizon widens round him, and the west
Looks vast with untracked waves whereon his
      gaze
Follows the flight of the swift-vanished bird
That like the sunken sun is mirrored still
Upon the yearning soul within the eye.
And so in Córdova through patient nights
Columbus watches, or he sails in dreams
Between the setting stars and finds new day ;
Then wakes again to the old weary days,
Girds on the cord and frock of pale Saint Fran-
      cis,
And like him zealous pleads with foolish men.
" I ask but for a million maravedis :
Give me three caravels to find a world,
New shores, new realms, new soldiers for the
      Cross·

Son cosas grandes !" Thus he pleads in vain ;
Yet faints not utterly, but pleads anew,
Thinking, " God means it, and has chosen me."
For this man is the pulse of all mankind
Feeding an embryo future, offspring strange
Of the fond Present, that with mother-prayers
And mother-fancies looks for championship
Of all her loved beliefs and old-world ways
From that young Time she bears within her
    womb.
The sacred places shall be purged again,
The Turk converted, and the Holy Church,
Like the mild Virgin with the outspread robe,
Shall fold all tongues and nations lovingly.

But since God works by armies, who shall be
The modern Cyrus? Is it France most Christian,
Who with his lilies and brocaded knights,
French oaths, French vices, and the newest style
Of out-puffed sleeve, shall pass from west to east,
A winnowing fan to purify the seed
For fair millennial harvests soon to come?
Or is not Spain the land of chosen warriors ?—
Crusaders consecrated from the womb,
Carrying the sword-cross stamped upon their
    souls
By the long yearnings of a nation's life,
Through all the seven patient centuries
Since first Pelayo and his resolute band
Trusted the God within their Gothic hearts
At Covadunga, and defied Mahound ;
Beginning so the Holy War of Spain
That now is panting with the eagerness
Of labor near its end.   The silver cross
Glitters o'er Malaga and streams dread light
On Moslem galleys, turning all their stores
From threats to gifts.   What Spanish knight is he

Who, living now, holds it not shame to live
Apart from that hereditary battle
Which needs his sword? Castilian gentlemen
Choose not their task—they choose to do it well.

The time is great, and greater no man's trust
Than his who keeps the fortress for his king,
Wearing great honors as some delicate robe
Brocaded o'er with names 'twere sin to tarnish.
Born de la Cerda, Calatravan knight,
Count of Segura, fourth Duke of Bedmár,
Offshoot from that high stock of old Castile
Whose topmost branch is proud Medina Celi—
Such titles with their blazonry are his
Who keeps this fortress, its sworn governor,
Lord of the valley, master of the town,
Commanding whom he will, himself commanded
By Christ his Lord who sees him from the Cross
And from bright heaven where the Mother
        pleads ;—
By good Saint James upon the milk-white steed,
Who leaves his bliss to fight for chosen Spain ;—
By the dead gaze of all his ancestors ;—
And by the mystery of his Spanish blood
Charged with the awe and glories of the past.

See now with soldiers in his front and rear
He winds at evening through the narrow streets
That toward the Castle gate climb devious :
His charger, of fine Andalusian stock,
An Indian beauty, black but delicate,
Is conscious of the herald trumpet note,
The gathering glances, and familiar ways
That lead fast homeward : she forgets fatigue,
And at the light touch of the master's spur
Thrills with the zeal to bear him royally,
Arches her neck and clambers up the stones

As if disdainful of the difficult steep.
Night-black the charger, black the rider's plume,
But all between is bright with morning hues—
Seems ivory and gold and deep blue gems,
And starry flashing steel and pale vermilion,
All set in jasper : on his surcoat white
Glitter the sword-belt and the jewelled hilt,
Red on the back and breast the holy cross,
And 'twixt the helmet and the soft-spun white
Thick tawny wavelets like the lion's mane
Turn backward from his brow, pale, wide, erect,
Shadowing blue eyes—blue as the rain-washed
          sky
That braced the early stem of Gothic kings
He claims for ancestry.   A goodly knight,
A noble caballero, broad of chest
And long of limb.   So much the August sun,
Now in the west but shooting half its beams
Past a dark rocky profile toward the plain,
At windings of the path across the slope
Makes suddenly luminous for all who see :
For women smiling from the terraced roofs ;
For boys that prone on trucks with head up-
          propped
Lazy and curious, stare irreverent ;
For men who make obeisance with degrees
Of good-will shading toward servility,
Where good-will ends and secret fear begins
And curses, too, low-muttered through the teeth,
Explanatory to the God of Shem.

Five, grouped within a whitened tavern court
Of Moorish fashion, where the trellised vines
Purpling above their heads make odorous shade,
Note through the open door the passers-by,
Getting some rills of novelty to speed
The lagging stream of talk and help the wine.

'Tis Christian to drink wine : whoso denies
His flesh at bidding save of Holy Church,
Let him beware and take to Christian sins
Lest he be taxed with Moslem sanctity.

The souls are five, the talkers only three.
(No time, most tainted by wrong faith and rule,
But holds some listeners and dumb animals.)
MINE HOST is one : he with the well-arched nose,
Soft-eyed, fat-handed, loving men for nought
But his own humor, patting old and young
Upon the back, and mentioning the cost
With confidential blandness, as a tax
That he collected much against his will
From Spaniards who were all his bosom friends :
Warranted Christian—else how keep an inn,
Which calling asks true faith ? though like his
        wine
Of cheaper sort, a trifle over-new.
His father was a convert, chose the chrism
As men choose physic, kept his chimney warm
With smokiest wood upon a Saturday,
Counted his gains and grudges on a chaplet,
And crossed himself asleep for fear of spies ;
Trusting the God of Israel would see
'Twas Christian tyranny that made him base.
Our host his son was born ten years too soon,
Had heard his mother call him Ephraim,
Knew holy things from common, thought it sin
To feast on days when Israel's children mourned,
So had to be converted with his sire,
To doff the awe he learned as Ephraim,
And suit his manners to a Christian name.
But infant awe, that unborn moving thing,
Dies with what nourished it, can never rise
From the dead womb and walk and seek new
        pasture.

Thus baptism seemed to him a merry game
Not tried before, all sacraments a mode
Of doing homage for one's property,
And all religions a queer human whim
Or else a vice, according to degrees :
As, 'tis a whim to like your chestnuts hot,
Burn your own mouth and draw your face awry,
A vice to pelt frogs with them—animals
Content to take life coolly.   And Lorenzo
Would have all lives made easy, even lives
Of spiders and inquisitors, yet still
Wishing so well to flies and Moors and Jews
He rather wished the others easy death ;
For loving all men clearly was deferred
Till all men loved each other.   Such mine Host,
With chiselled smile caressing Seneca,
The solemn mastiff leaning on his knee.

His right-hand guest is solemn as the dog,
Square-faced and massive : BLASCO is his name,
A prosperous silversmith from Aragon ;
In speech not silvery, rather tuned as notes
From a deep vessel made of plenteous iron,
Or some great bell of slow but certain swing
That, if you only wait, will tell the hour
As well as flippant clocks that strike in haste
And set off chiming a superfluous tune—
Like JUAN there, the spare man with the lute,
Who makes you dizzy with his rapid tongue,
Whirring athwart your mind with comment swift
On speech you would have finished by-and-by,
Shooting your bird for you while you are loading,
Cheapening your wisdom as a pattern known,
Woven by any shuttle on demand.
Can never sit quite still, too : sees a wasp
And kills it with a movement like a flash ;
Whistles low notes or seems to thrum his lute

As a mere hyphen 'twixt two syllables
Of any steadier man ; walks up and down
And snuffs the orange flowers and shoots a pea
To hit a streak of light let through the awning.
Has a queer face : eyes large as plums, a nose
Small, round, uneven, like a bit of wax
Melted and cooled by chance.   Thin-fingered,
        lithe,
And as a squirrel noiseless, startling men
Only by quickness.   In his speech and look
A touch of graceful wildness, as of things
Not trained or tamed for uses of the world ;
Most like the Fauns that roamed in days of old
About the listening whispering woods, and
        shared
The subtler sense of sylvan ears and eyes
Undulled by scheming thought, yet joined the
        rout
Of men and women on the festal days,
And played the syrinx too, and knew love's
        pains,
Turning their anguish into melody.
For Juan was a minstrel still, in times
When minstrelsy was held a thing outworn.
Spirits seem buried and their epitaph
Is writ in Latin by severest pens,
Yet still they flit above the trodden grave
And find new bodies, animating them
In quaint and ghostly way with antique souls.
So Juan was a troubadour revived,
Freshening life's dusty road with babbling rills
Of wit and song, living 'mid harnessed men
With limbs ungalled by armor, ready so
To soothe them weary, and to cheer them sad.
Guest at the board, companion in the camp,
A crystal mirror to the life around,
Flashing the comment keen of simple fact

Defined in words ; lending brief lyric voice
To grief and sadness ; hardly taking note
Of difference betwixt his own and others';
But rather singing as a listener
To the deep moans, the cries, the wild strong joys
Of universal Nature, old yet young.
Such Juan, the third talker, shimmering bright
As butterfly or bird with quickest life.
The silent ROLDAN has his brightness too,
But only in his spangles and rosettes.
His parti-colored vest and crimson hose
Are dulled with old Valencian dust, his eyes
With straining fifty years at gilded balls
To catch them dancing, or with brazen looks
At men and women as he made his jests
Some thousand times and watched to count the
        pence
His wife was gathering.   His olive face
Has an old writing in it, characters
Stamped deep by grins that had no merriment,
The soul's rude mark proclaiming all its blank ;
As on some faces that have long grown old
In lifting tapers up to forms obscene
On ancient walls and chuckling with false zest
To please my lord, who gives the larger fee
For that hard industry in apishness.
Roldan would gladly never laugh again ;
Pensioned, he would be grave as any ox,
And having beans and crumbs and oil secured
Would borrow no man's jokes for evermore.
'Tis harder now because his wife is gone,
Who had quick feet, and danced to ravishment
Of every ring jewelled with Spanish eyes,
But died and left this boy, lame from his birth,
And sad and obstinate, though when he will
He sings God-taught such marrow-thrilling
        strains

As seem the very voice of dying Spring,
A flute-like wail that mourns the blossoms gone,
And sinks, and is not, like their fragrant breath,
With fine transition on the trembling air.
He sits as if imprisoned by some fear,
Motionless, with wide eyes that seem not made
For hungry glancing of a twelve-year'd boy
To mark the living thing that he could tease,
But for the gaze of some primeval sadness
Dark twin with light in the creative ray.
This little PABLO has his spangles too,
And large rosettes to hide his poor left foot
Rounded like any hoof (his mother thought
God willed it so to punish all her sins).

I said the souls were five—besides the dog.
But there was still a sixth, with wrinkled face,
Grave and disgusted with all merriment
Not less than Roldan.   It is ANNIBAL,
The experienced monkey who performs the
        tricks,
Jumps through the hoops, and carries round the
        hat.
Once full of sallies and impromptu feats,
Now cautious not to light on aught that's new,
Lest he be whipped to do it o'er again
From A to Z, and make the gentry laugh :
A misanthropic monkey, gray and grim,
Bearing a lot that has no remedy
For want of concert in the monkey tribe.

We see the company, above their heads
The braided matting, golden as ripe corn,
Stretched in a curving strip close by the grapes,
Elsewhere rolled back to greet the cooler sky ;
A fountain near, vase-shapen and broad-lipped,
Where timorous birds alight with tiny feet,

And hesitate and bend wise listening ears,
And fly away again with undipped beak.
On the stone floor the juggler's heaped-up goods,
Carpet and hoops, viol and tambourine,
Where Annibal sits perched with brows severe,
A serious ape whom none take seriously,
Obliged in this fool's world to earn his nuts
By hard buffoonery.   We see them all,
And hear their talk—the talk of Spanish men,
With southern intonation, vowels turned
Caressingly between the consonants,
Persuasive, willing, with such intervals
As music borrows from the wooing birds,
That plead with subtly curving, sweet descent—
And yet can quarrel, as hese Spaniards can.

JUAN (*near the doorway*).

You hear the trumpet? There's old Ramon's
    blast.
No bray but his can shake the air so well.
He takes his trumpeting as solemnly
As angel charged to wake the dead ; thinks war
Was made for trumpeters, and their great art
Made solely for themselves who understand it.
His features all have shaped themselves to blow-
    ing,
And when his trumpet's bagged or left at home
He seems a chattel in a broker's booth,
A spoutless watering-can, a promise to pay
No sum particular.   O fine old Ramon !
The blasts get louder and the clattering hoofs ;
They crack the ear as well as heaven's thunder
For owls that listen blinking.   There's the
    banner.

HOST (*joining him : the others follow to the door*).

The Duke has finished reconnoitring, then ?

We shall hear news. They say he means a
      sally—
Would strike El Zagal's Moors as they push
      home
Like ants with booty heavier than themselves;
Then, joined by other nobles with their bands,
Lay siege to Guadix. Juan, you're a bird
That nest within the Castle. What say you?

JUAN.

Nought, I say nought. 'Tis but a toilsome game
To bet upon that feather Policy,
And guess where after twice a hundred puffs
'Twill catch another feather crossing it:
Guess how the Pope will blow and how the king;
What force my lady's fan has; how a cough
Seizing the Padre's throat may raise a gust,
And how the queen may sigh the feather down.
Such catching at imaginary threads,
Such spinning twisted air, is not for me.
If I should want a game, I'll rather bet
On racing snails, two large, slow, lingering
      snails—
No spurring, equal weights—a chance sublime,
Nothing to guess at, pure uncertainty.
Here comes the Duke. They give but feeble
      shouts,
And some look sour.

HOST.

      That spoils a fair occasion.
Civility brings no conclusions with it,
And cheerful *Vivas* make the moments glide
Instead of grating like a rusty wheel.

JUAN.

O they are dullards, kick because they're stung,
And bruise a friend to show they hate a wasp.

HOST.

Best treat your wasp with delicate regard ;
When the right moment comes say, "By your
    leave,"
Use your heel—so ! and make an end of him.
That's if we talked of wasps ; but our young
    Duke—
Spain holds not a more gallant gentleman.
Live, live, Duke Silva ! 'Tis a rare smile he has,
But seldom seen.

JUAN.

A true hidalgo's smile,
That gives much favor, but beseeches none.
His smile is sweetened by his gravity :
It comes like dawn upon Sierra snows,
Seeming more generous for the coldness gone ;
Breaks from the calm—a sudden opening flower
On dark deep waters : now a chalice shut,
A mystic shrine, the next a full-rayed star,
Thrilling, pulse-quickening as a living word.
I'll make a song of that.

HOST.

Prithee, not now.
You'll fall to staring like a wooden saint,
And wag your head as it were set on wires.
Here's fresh sherbet.   Sit, be good company.
(*To* BLASCO) You are a stranger, sir, and cannot
    know
How our Duke's nature suits his princely frame.

BLASCO.

Nay, but I marked his spurs—chased cunningly !
A duke should know good gold and silver plate ;
Then he will know the quality of mine.
I've ware for tables and for altars too,
Our Lady in all sizes, crosses, bells :

He'll need such weapons full as much as swords
If he would capture any Moorish town.
For, let me tell you, when a mosque is cleansed . . .

JUAN.

The demons fly so thick from sound of bells
And smell of incense, you may see the air
Streaked with them as with smoke.   Why, they
    are spirits:
You may well think how crowded they must be
To make a sort of haze.

BLASCO.

                I knew not that.
Still they're of smoky nature, demons are;
And since you say so—well, it proves the more
The need of bells and censers.   Ay, your Duke
Sat well: a true hidalgo.   I can judge—
Of harness specially.   I saw the camp,
The royal camp at Velez Malaga.
'Twas like the court of heaven—such liveries!
And torches carried by the score at night
Before the nobles.   Sirs, I made a dish
To set an emerald in would fit a crown,
For Don Alonzo, lord of Aguilar.
Your Duke's no whit behind him in his mien
Or harness either.   But you seem to say
The people love him not.

HOST.

             They've nought against him.
But certain winds will make men's temper bad.
When the Solano blows hot venomed breath,
It acts upon men's knives: steel takes to stab-
    bing
Which else, with cooler winds, were honest steel,
Cutting but garlic.   There's a wind just now
Blows right from Seville—

BLASCO.

     Ay, you mean the wind . . .
Yes, yes, a wind that's rather hot . . .

HOST.

              With fagots.

JUAN.

A wind that suits not with our townsmen's blood.
Abram, 'tis said, objected to be scorched,
And, as the learned Arabs vouch, he gave
The antipathy in full to Ishmaël.
'Tis true, these patriarchs had their oddities.

BLASCO.

Their oddities? I'm of their mind, I know.
Though, as to Abraham and Ishmaël,
I'm an old Christian, and owe nought to them
Or any Jew among them. But I know
We made a stir in Saragossa—we :
The men of Aragon ring hard—true metal.
Sirs, I'm no friend to heresy, but then
A Christian's money is not safe. As how?
A lapsing Jew or any heretic
May owe me twenty ounces : suddenly
He's prisoned, suffers penalties—'tis well :
If men will not believe, 'tis good to make them,
But let the penalties fall on them alone.
The Jew is stripped, his goods are confiscate ;
Now, where, I pray you, go my twenty ounces ?
God knows, and perhaps the King may, but not I.
And more, my son may lose his young wife's
     dower
Because 'twas promised since her father's soul
Fell to wrong thinking. How was I to know ?
I could but use my sense and cross myself.
Christian is Christian—I give in—but still
Taxing is taxing, though you call it holy.

We Saragossans liked not this new tax
They call the—nonsense, I'm from Aragon !
I speak too bluntly.   But for Holy Church,
No man believes more.

HOST.
                              Nay, sir, never fear.
Good Master Roldan here is no delator.

ROLDAN (*starting from a reverie*).
You speak to me, sirs ?   I perform to-night—
The Plaça Santiago.   Twenty tricks,
All different.   I dance, too.   And the boy
Sings like a bird.   I crave your patronage.

BLASCO.
Faith, you shall have it, sir.   In travelling
I take a little freedom, and am gay.
You marked not what I said just now?

ROLDAN.
                                        I ? no.
I pray your pardon.   I've a twinging knee,
That makes it hard to listen.   You were saying?

BLASCO.
Nay, it was nought.   (*Aside to* HOST) Is it his
      deepness?
                    HOST.
                              No.
He's deep in nothing but his poverty.

BLASCO.
But 'twas his poverty that made me think . . .

HOST.
His piety might wish to keep the feasts
As well as fasts.   No fear ; he hears not.

BLASCO.

Good.

I speak my mind about the penalties,
But, look you, I'm against assassination.
You know my meaning—Master Arbués,
The grand Inquisitor in Aragon.
I knew nought—paid no copper toward the deed.
But I was there, at prayers, within the church.
How could I help it ?   Why, the saints were there,
And looked straight on above the altars. I . . .

JUAN.

Looked carefully another way.

BLASCO.

Why, at my beads.
'Twas after midnight, and the canons all
Were chanting matins.   I was not in church
To gape and stare.   I saw the martyr kneel :
I never liked the look of him alive—
He was no martyr then.   I thought he made
An ugly shadow as he crept athwart
The bands of light, then passed within the gloom
By the broad pillar.   'Twas in our great Seo,
At Saragossa.   The pillars tower so large
You cross yourself to see them, lest white Death
Should hide behind their dark.   And so it was.
I looked away again and told my beads
Unthinkingly ; but still a man has ears ;
And right across the chanting came a sound
As if a tree had crashed above the roar
Of some great torrent.   So it seemed to me ;
For when you listen long and shut your eyes
Small sounds get thunderous.   He had a shell
Like any lobster : a good iron suit
From top to toe beneath the innocent serge.
That made the tell-tale sound.   But then came
        shrieks.

The chanting stopped and turned to rushing feet,
And in the midst lay Master Arbués,
Felled like an ox.   'Twas wicked butchery.
Some honest men had hoped it would have scared
The Inquisition out of Aragon.
'Twas money thrown away—I would say, crime—
Clean thrown away.

HOST.

     That was a pity now.
Next to a missing thrust, what irks me most
Is a neat well-aimed stroke that kills your man,
Yet ends in mischief—as in Aragon.
It was a lesson to our people here.
Else there's a monk within our city walls,
A holy, high-born, stern Dominican,
They might have made the great mistake to kill.

BLASCO.

What ! is he ? . . .

HOST.

     Yes ; a Master Arbués
Of finer quality.   The Prior here
And uncle to our Duke.

BLASCO.

     He will want plate :
A holy pillar or a crucifix.
But, did you say, he was like Arbués ?

JUAN.

As a black eagle with gold beak and claws
Is like a raven.   Even in his cowl,
Covered from head to foot, the Prior is known
From all the black herd round.   When he un-
  covers
And stands white-frocked, with ivory face, his
  eyes

Black-gleaming, black his coronal of hair
Like shredded jasper, he seems less a man
With struggling aims, than pure incarnate Will,
Fit to subdue rebellious nations, nay,
That human flesh he breathes in, charged with
      passion
Which quivers in his nostril and his lip,
But disciplined by long in-dwelling will
To silent labor in the yoke of law.
A truce to thy comparisons, Lorenzo !
Thine is no subtle nose for difference ;
'Tis dulled by feigning and civility.

HOST.

Pooh, thou'rt a poet, crazed with finding words
May stick to things and seem like qualities.
No pebble is a pebble in thy hands :
'Tis a moon out of work, a barren egg,
Or twenty things that no man sees but thee.
Our Father Isidor's—a living saint,
And that is heresy, some townsmen think :
Saints should be dead, according to the Church.
My mind is this : the Father is so holy
'Twere sin to wish his soul detained from bliss.
Easy translation to the realms above,
The shortest journey to the seventh heaven,
Is what I'd never grudge him.

BLASCO.

                Piously said.
Look you, I'm dutiful, obey the Church
When there's no help for it : I mean to say,
When Pope and Bishop and all customers
Order alike.   But there be bishops now,
And were aforetime, who have held it wrong,
This hurry to convert the Jews.   As how ?
Your Jew pays tribute to the bishop, say.

That's good, and must please God, to see the
    Church
Maintained in ways that ease the Christian's
    purse.
Convert the Jew, and where's the tribute, pray?
He lapses, too: 'tis slippery work, conversion:
And then the holy taxing carries off
His money at one sweep.   No tribute more!
He's penitent or burnt, and there's an end.
Now guess which pleases God . . .

           JUAN.
                        Whether he likes
A well-burnt Jew or well-fed bishop best.

[While Juan put this problem theologic
Entered, with resonant step, another guest—
A soldier: all his keenness in his sword,
His eloquence in scars upon his cheek,
His virtue in much slaying of the Moor:
With brow well-creased in horizontal folds
To save the space, as having nought to do:
Lips prone to whistle whisperingly—no tune,
But trotting rhythm: meditative eyes,
Most often fixed upon his legs and spurs:
Styled Captain Lopez.]

           LOPEZ.
              At your service, sirs.

           JUAN.
Ha, Lopez? Why, thou hast a face full-charged
As any herald's.   What news of the wars?

           LOPEZ.
Such news as is most bitter on my tongue.

           JUAN.
Then spit it forth.

HOST.

      Sit, Captain : here's a cup,
Fresh-filled.   What news ?

LOPEZ.

      'Tis bad.   We make no sally :
We sit still here and wait whate'er the Moor
Shall please to do.

HOST.

      Some townsmen will be glad.

LOPEZ.

Glad, will they be ?   But I'm not glad, not I,
Nor any Spanish soldier of clean blood.
But the Duke's wisdom is to wait a siege
Instead of laying one.   Therefore—meantime—
He will be married straightway.

HOST.

      Ha, ha, ha !
Thy speech is like an hourglass ; turn it down
The other way, 'twill stand as well, and say
The Duke will wed, therefore he waits a siege.
But what say Don Diego and the Prior ?
The holy uncle and the fiery Don ?

LOPEZ.

O there be sayings running all abroad
As thick as nuts o'erturned.   No man need lack.
Some say, 'twas letters changed the Duke's in-
    tent :
From Malaga, says Blas.   From Rome, says
    Quintin.
From spies at Guadix, says Sebastian.
Some say, 'tis all a pretext—say, the Duke
Is but a lapdog hanging on a skirt,
Turning his eyeballs upward like a monk :

'Twas Don Diego said that—so says Blas ;
Last week, he said . . .

JUAN.

O do without the "said !"
Open thy mouth and pause in lieu of it.
I had as lief be pelted with a pea
Irregularly in the self-same spot
As hear such iteration without rule,
Such torture of uncertain certainty.

LOPEZ.

Santiago ! Juan, thou art hard to please.
I speak not for my own delighting, I.
I can be silent, I.

BLASCO.

Nay, sir, speak on !
I like your matter well.   I deal in plate.
This wedding touches me.   Who is the bride ?

LOPEZ.

One that some say the Duke does ill to wed.
One that his mother reared — God rest her
       soul !—
Duchess Diana—she who died last year.
A bird picked up away from any nest.
Her name—the Duchess gave it—is Fedalma.
No harm in that.   But the Duke stoops, they
       say,
In wedding her.   And that's the simple truth.

JUAN.

Thy simple truth is but a false opinion :
The simple truth of asses who believe
Their thistle is the very best of food.
Fie, Lopez, thou a Spaniard with a sword
Dreamest a Spanish noble ever stoops

By doing honor to the maid he loves !
He stoops alone when he dishonors her.

LOPEZ.

Nay, I said nought against her.

JUAN.

               Better not.
Else I would challenge thee to fight with wits,
And spear thee through and through ere thou
     couldst draw
The bluntest word.   Yes, yes, consult thy spurs :
Spurs are a sign of knighthood, and should tell
     thee
That knightly love is blent with reverence
As heavenly air is blent with heavenly blue.
Don Silva's heart beats to a loyal tune :
He wills no highest-born Castilian dame,
Betrothed to highest noble, should be held
More sacred than Fedalma.   He enshrines
Her virgin image for the general awe
And for his own—will guard her from the world,
Nay, his profaner self, lest he should lose
The place of his religion.   He does well.
Nought can come closer to the poet's strain.

HOST.

Or farther from his practice, Juan, eh ?
If thou'rt a sample ?

JUAN.

           Wrong there, my Lorenzo !
Touching Fedalma the poor poet plays
A finer part even than the noble Duke.

LOPEZ.

By making ditties, singing with round mouth
Likest a crowing cock?   Thou meanest that?

JUAN.

Lopez, take physic, thou art getting ill,
Growing descriptive ; 'tis unnatural.
I mean, Don Silva's love expects reward,
Kneels with a heaven to come ; but the poor poet
Worships without reward, nor hopes to find
A heaven save in his worship.   He adores
The sweetest woman for her sweetness' sake,
Joys in the love that was not born for him,
Because 'tis lovingness, as beggars joy,
Warming their naked limbs on wayside walls,
To hear a tale of princes and their glory.
There's a poor poet (poor, I mean, in coin)
Worships Fedalma with so true a love
That if her silken robe were changed for rags,
And she were driven out to stony wilds
Barefoot, a scornéd wanderer, he would kiss
Her ragged garment's edge, and only ask
For leave to be her slave.   Digest that, friend,
Or let it lie upon thee as a weight
To check light thinking of Fedalma.

LOPEZ.

I ?

I think no harm of her ; I thank the saints
I wear a sword and peddle not in thinking.
'Tis Father Marcos says she'll not confess
And loves not holy water ; says her blood
Is infidel ; says the Duke's wedding her
Is union of light with darkness.

JUAN.

Tush !

[Now Juan—who by snatches touched his lute
With soft arpeggio, like a whispered dream
Of sleeping music, while he spoke of love—
In jesting anger at the soldier's talk

Thrummed loud and fast, then faster and more
    loud,
Till, as he answered " Tush ! " he struck a chord
Sudden as whip-crack close by Lopez' ear.
Mine host and Blasco smiled, the mastiff barked,
Roldan looked up and Annibal looked down,
Cautiously neutral in so new a case ;
The boy raised longing, listening eyes that seemed
An exiled spirit's waiting in strained hope
Of voices coming from the distant land.
But Lopez bore the assault like any rock :
That was not what he drew his sword at—he !
He spoke with neck erect.]

LOPEZ.

                If that's a hint
The company should ask thee for a song.
Sing, then !

HOST.

          Ay, Juan, sing, and jar no more.
Something brand new.   Thou'rt wont to make
    my ear
A test of novelties.   Hast thou aught fresh ?

JUAN.

As fresh as rain-drops.   Here's a Cancion
Springs like a tiny mushroom delicate
Out of the priest's foul scandal of Fedalma.

[He preluded with querying intervals,
Rising, then falling just a semitone,
In minor cadence—sound with poiséd wing
Hovering and quivering toward the needed fall.
Then in a voice that shook the willing air
With masculine vibration sang this song.

Should I long that dark were fair?
Say, O song!
Lacks my love aught, that I should long?

Dark the night, with breath all flow'rs,
And tender broken voice that fills
 With ravishment the listening hours:
Whisperings, wooings,
Liquid ripples and soft ring-dove cooings
In low-toned rhythm that love's aching stills.
Dark the night,
 Yet is she bright,
For in her dark she brings the mystic star,
 Trembling yet strong, as is the voice of love,
From some unknown afar.
O radiant Dark! O darkly-fostered ray!
 Thou hast a joy too deep for shallow Day.

While Juan sang, all round the tavern court
Gathered a constellation of black eyes.
Fat Lola leaned upon the balcony
With arms that might have pillowed Hercules
(Who built, 'tis known, the mightiest Spanish
        towns);
Thin Alda's face, sad as a wasted passion,
Leaned o'er the nodding baby's; 'twixt the rails
The little Pepe showed his two black beads,
His flat-ringed hair and small Semitic nose,
Complete and tiny as a new-born minnow;
Patting his head and holding in her arms
The baby senior, stood Lorenzo's wife
All negligent, her kerchief discomposed
By little clutches, woman's coquetry
Quite turned to mother's cares and sweet content.
These on the balcony, while at the door
Gazed the lank boys and lazy-shouldered men.
'Tis likely too the rats and insects peeped,

Being southern Spanish ready for a lounge.
The singer smiled, as doubtless Orpheus smiled,
To see the animals both great and small,
The mountainous elephant and scampering mouse,
Held by the ears in decent audience ;
Then, when mine host desired the strain once
     more,
He fell to preluding with rhythmic change
Of notes recurrent, soft as pattering drops
That fall from off the eaves in faëry dance
When clouds are breaking ; till at measured
     pause
He struck with strength, in rare responsive
     chords.]

HOST.

Come, then, a gayer ballad, if thou wilt :
I quarrel not with change.   What say you, Cap-
     tain ?

LOPEZ.

All's one to me.   I note no change of tune,
Not I, save in the ring of horses' hoofs,
Or in the drums and trumpets when they call
To action or retreat.   I ne'er could see
The good of singing.

BLASCO.

        Why, it passes time—
Saves you from getting over-wise : that's good.
For, look you, fools are merry here below,
Yet they will go to heaven all the same,
Having the sacraments ; and, look you, heaven
Is a long holiday, and solid men,
Used to much business, might be ill at ease
Not liking play.   And so, in travelling,
I shape myself betimes to idleness
And take fools' pleasures . . .

HOST.

    Hark, the song begins!

JUAN (*sings*).

Maiden, crowned with glossy blackness,
 Lithe as panther forest-roaming,
Long-armed naiad, when she dances,
 On a stream of ether floating—
   Bright, O bright Fedalma!

Form all curves like softness drifted,
 Wave-kissed marble roundly dimpling,
Far-off music slowly wingèd,
 Gently rising, gently sinking—
   Bright, O bright Fedalma!

Pure as rain-tear on a rose-leaf,
 Cloud high-born in noonday spotless,
Sudden perfect as the dew-bead,
 Gem of earth and sky begotten—
   Bright, O bright Fedalma!

Beauty has no mortal father,
 Holy light her form engendered
Out of tremor, yearning, gladness,
 Presage sweet and joy remembered—
   Child of Light, Fedalma!

BLASCO.

Faith, a good song, sung to a stirring tune.
I like the words returning in a round;
It gives a sort of sense. Another such!

ROLDAN (*rising*).

Sirs, you will hear my boy. 'Tis very hard
When gentles sing for nought to all the town.
How can a poor man live? And now 'tis time
I go to the Plaça—who will give me pence
When he can hear hidalgos and give nought?

JUAN.

True, friend. Be pacified. I'll sing no more.
Go thou, and we will follow. Never fear.
My voice is common as the ivy-leaves,
Plucked in all seasons—bears no price ; thy boy's
Is like the almond blossoms. Ah, he's lame !

HOST.

Load him not heavily. Here, Pedro ! help.
Go with them to the Plaça, take the hoops.
The sights will pay thee.

BLASCO.

         I'll be there anon,
And set the fashion with a good white coin.
But let us see as well as hear.

HOST.

         Ay, prithee.
Some tricks, a dance.

BLASCO.

         Yes, 'tis more rational.

ROLDAN (*turning round with the bundle and
monkey on his shoulders*).

You shall see all, sirs. There's no man in Spain
Knows his art better. I've a twinging knee
Oft hinders dancing, and the boy is lame.
But no man's monkey has more tricks than mine.

[At this high praise the gloomy Annibal,
Mournful professor of high drollery,
Seemed to look gloomier, and the little troop
Went slowly out, escorted from the door
By all the idlers. From the balcony
Slowly subsided the black radiance
Of agate eyes, and broke in chattering sounds,

Coaxings and trampings, and the small hoarse
    squeak
Of Pepe's reed.   And our group talked again.]

HOST.

I'll get this juggler, if he quits him well,
An audience here as choice as can be lured.
For me, when a poor devil does his best,
'Tis my delight to soothe his soul with praise.
What though the best be bad? remains the good
Of throwing food to a lean hungry dog.
I'd give up the best jugglery in life
To see a miserable juggler pleased.
But that's my humor.   Crowds are malcontent
And cruel as the Holy . . . . Shall we go?
All of us now together?

LOPEZ.
           Well, not I.
I may be there anon, but first I go
To the lower prison.   There is strict command
That all our gypsy prisoners shall to-night
Be lodged within the fort.   They've forged
    enough
Of balls and bullets—used up all the metal.
At morn to-morrow they must carry stones
Up the south tower.   'Tis a fine stalwart band,
Fit for the hardest tasks.   Some say, the queen
Would have the Gypsies banished with the Jews.
Some say, 'twere better harness them for work.
They'd feed on any filth and save the Spaniard.
Some say—but I must go.   'Twill soon be time
To head the escort.   We shall meet again.

BLASCO.

Go, sir, with God (*exit Lopez*).   A very proper
    man,
And soldierly.   But, for this banishment

Some men are hot on, it ill pleases me.
The Jews, now (sirs, if any Christian here
Had Jews for ancestors, I blame him not ;
We cannot all be Goths of Aragon)—
Jews are not fit for heaven, but on earth
They are most useful.   'Tis the same with mules,
Horses, or oxen, or with any pig
Except Saint Anthony's.   They are useful here
(The Jews, I mean) though they may go to hell.
And, look you, useful sins—why Providence
Sends Jews to do 'em, saving Christian souls.
The very Gypsies, curbed and harnessed well,
Would make draught cattle, feed on vermin too,
Cost less than grazing brutes, and turn bad food
To handsome carcasses ; sweat at the forge
For little wages, and well drilled and flogged
Might work like slaves, some Spaniards looking
        on.
I deal in plate, and am no priest to say
What God may mean, save when he means plain
        sense ;
But when he sent the Gypsies wandering
In punishment because they sheltered not
Our Lady and Saint Joseph (and no doubt
Stole the small ass they fled with into Egypt),
Why send them here ?   'Tis plain he saw the use
They'd be to Spaniards.   Shall we banish them,
And tell God we know better ?   'Tis a sin.
They talk of vermin ; but, sirs, vermin large
Were made to eat the small, or else to eat
The noxious rubbish, and picked Gypsy men
Might serve in war to climb, be killed, and fall
To make an easy ladder.   Once I saw
A Gypsy sorcerer, at a spring and grasp
Kill one who came to seize him : talk of strength !
Nay, swiftness too, for while we crossed ourselves
He vanished like—say, like . . .

JUAN.

        A swift black snake,
Or like a living arrow fledged with will.

BLASCO.

Why, did you see him, pray ?

JUAN.

          Not then, but now,
As painters see the many in the one.
We have a Gypsy in Bedmár whose frame
Nature compacted with such fine selection,
'Twould yield a dozen types : all Spanish knights,
From him who slew Rolando at the pass
Up to the mighty Cid ; all deities,
Thronging Olympus in fine attitudes ;
Or all hell's heroes whom the poet saw
Tremble like lions, writhe like demigods.

HOST.

Pause not yet, Juan—more hyperbole !
Shoot upward still and flare in meteors
Before thou sink to earth in dull brown fact.

BLASCO.

Nay, give me fact, high shooting suits not me.
I never stare to look for soaring larks.
What is this Gypsy ?

HOST.

        Chieftain of a band,
The Moor's allies, whom full a month ago
Our Duke surprised and brought as captives
      home.
He needed smiths, and doubtless the brave Moor
Has missed some useful scouts and archers too.
Juan's fantastic pleasure is to watch

These Gypsies forging, and to hold discourse
With this great chief, whom he transforms at
    will
To sage or warrior, and like the sun
Plays daily at fallacious alchemy,
Turns sand to gold and dewy spider-webs
To myriad rainbows.   Still the sand is sand,
And still in sober shade you see the web.
'Tis so, I'll wager, with his Gypsy chief—
A piece of stalwart cunning, nothing more.

JUAN.

No!   My invention had been all too poor
To frame this Zarca as I saw him first.
'Twas when they stripped him.   In his chief-
    tain's gear,
Amidst his men he seemed a royal barb
Followed by wild-maned Andalusian colts.
He had a necklace of a strange device
In finest gold of unknown workmanship,
But delicate as Moorish, fit to kiss
Fedalma's neck, and play in shadows there.
He wore fine mail, a rich-wrought sword and
    belt,
And on his surcoat black a broidered torch,
A pine-branch flaming, grasped by two dark
    hands.
But when they stripped him of his ornaments
It was the the baubles lost their grace, not he.
His eyes, his mouth, his nostril, all inspired
With scorn that mastered utterance of scorn,
With power to check all rage until it turned
To ordered force, unleashed on chosen prey—
It seemed the soul within him made his limbs
And made them grand.   The baubles were well
    gone.
He stood the more a king, when bared to man.

BLASCO.

Maybe.   But nakedness is bad for trade,
And is not decent.   Well-wrought metal, sir,
Is not a bauble.   Had you seen the camp,
The royal camp at Velez Malaga,
Ponce de Leon and the other dukes,
The king himself and all his thousand knights
For bodyguard, 'twould not have left you breath
To praise a Gypsy thus.   A man's a man ;
But when you see a king, you see the work
Of many thousand men.   King Ferdinand
Bears a fine presence, and hath proper limbs ;
But what though he were shrunken as a relic ?
You'd see the gold and gems that cased him o'er,
And all the pages round him in brocade,
And all the lords, themselves a sort of kings,
Doing him reverence.   That strikes an awe
Into a common man—especially
A judge of plate.

HOST.

               Faith, very wisely said.
Purge thy speech, Juan.   It is over-full
Of this same Gypsy.   Praise the Catholic King,
And come now, let us see the juggler's skill.

———

The Plaça Santiago.

'Tis daylight still, but now the golden cross
Uplifted by the angel on the dome
Stands rayless in calm color clear-defined
Against the northern blue ; from turrets high
The flitting splendor sinks with folded wing
Dark-hid till morning, and the battlements
Wear soft relenting whiteness mellowed o'er
By summers generous and winters bland.
Now in the east the distance casts its veil
And gazes with a deepening earnestness.

The old rain-fretted mountains in their robes
Of shadow-broken gray ; the rounded hills
Reddened with blood of Titans, whose huge
    limbs,
Entombed within, feed full the hardy flesh
Of cactus green and blue broad-sworded aloes ;
The cypress soaring black above the lines
Of white court-walls ; the jointed sugar-canes
Pale-golden with their feathers motionless
In the warm quiet :—all thought-teaching form
Utters itself in firm unshimmering hues.
For the great rock has screened the westering
    sun
That still on plains beyond streams vaporous
    gold
Among the branches ; and within Bedmár
Has come the time of sweet serenity
When color glows unglittering, and the soul
Of visible things shows silent happiness,
As that of lovers trusting though apart.
The ripe-cheeked fruits, the crimson-petalled
    flowers ;
The wingéd life that pausing seems a gem
Cunningly carven on the dark green leaf;
The face of man with hues supremely blent
To difference fine as of a voice 'mid sounds :—
Each lovely light dipped thing seems to emerge
Flushed gravely from baptismal sacrament.
All beauteous existence rests, yet wakes,
Lies still, yet conscious, with clear open eyes
And gentle breath and mild suffuséd joy.
'Tis day, but day that falls like melody
Repeated on a string with graver tones—
Tones such as linger in a long farewell.

The Plaça widens in the passive air—
The Plaça Santiago, where the church,

A mosque converted, shows an eyeless face
Red-checkered, faded, doing penance still—
Bearing with Moorish arch the imaged saint,
Apostle, baron, Spanish warrior,
Whose charger's hoofs trample the turbaned
　　dead,
Whose banner with the Cross, the bloody sword
Flashes athwart the Moslem's glazing eye,
And mocks his trust in Allah who forsakes.
Up to the church the Plaça gently slopes,
In shape most like the pious palmer's shell,
Girdled with low white houses ; high above
Tower the strong fortress and sharp-angled wall
And well-flanked castle gate.　From o'er the
　　roofs,
And from the shadowed pátios cool, there
　　spreads
The breath of flowers and aromatic leaves
Soothing the sense with bliss indefinite—
A baseless hope, a glad presentiment,
That curves the lip more softly, fills the eye
With more indulgent beam.　And so it soothes,
So gently sways the pulses of the crowd
Who make a zone about the central spot
Chosen by Roldan for his theatre.
Maids with arched eyebrows, delicate-pencilled,
　　dark,
Fold their round arms below the kerchief full ;
Men shoulder little girls ; and grandames gray,
But muscular still, hold babies on their arms ;
While mothers keep the stout-legged boys in
　　front
Against their skirts, as old Greek pictures show
The Glorious Mother with the Boy divine.
Youths keep the places for themselves, and roll
Large lazy eyes, and call recumbent dogs
(For reasons deep below the reach of thought).

The old men cough with purpose, wish to hint
Wisdom within that cheapens jugglery,
Maintain a neutral air, and knit their brows
In observation.   None are quarrelsome,
Noisy, or very merry ; for their blood
Moves slowly into fervor—they rejoice
Like those dark birds that sweep with heavy
　　　wing,
Cheering their mates with melancholy cries.

But now the gilded balls begin to play
In rhythmic numbers, ruled by practice fine
Of eye and muscle : all the juggler's form
Consents harmonious in swift-gliding change,
Easily forward stretched or backward bent
With lightest step and movement circular
Round a fixed point : 'tis not the old Roldan
　　　now,
The dull, hard, weary, miserable man,
The soul all parched to languid appetite
And memory of desire : 'tis wondrous force
That moves in combination multiform
Toward conscious ends : 'tis Roldan glorious,
Holding all eyes like any meteor,
King of the moment save when Annibal
Divides the scene and plays the comic part,
Gazing with blinking glances up and down,
Dancing and throwing nought and catching it,
With mimicry as merry as the tasks
Of penance-working shades in Tartarus.

Pablo stands passive, and a space apart,
Holding a viol, waiting for command.
Music must not be wasted, but must rise
As needed climax ; and the audience
Is growing with late comers.   Juan now,
And the familiar Host, with Blasco broad,

Find way made gladly to the inmost round
Studded with heads.   Lorenzo knits the crowd
Into one family by showing all
Good-will and recognition.   Juan casts
His large and rapid measuring glance around ;
But—with faint quivering, transient as a breath
Shaking a flame—his eyes make sudden pause
Where by the jutting angle of a street
Castle-ward leading, stands a female form,
A kerchief pale square-drooping o'er the brow,
About her shoulders dim brown serge—in garb
Most like a peasant woman from the vale,
Who might have lingered after marketing
To see the show.   What thrill mysterious,
Ray-borne from orb to orb of conscious eyes,
The swift observing sweep of Juan's glance
Arrests an instant, then with prompting fresh
Diverts it lastingly ?   He turns at once
To watch the gilded balls, and nod and smile
At little round Pepíta, blondest maid
In all Bedmár—Pepíta, fair yet flecked,
Saucy of lip and nose, of hair as red
As breasts of robins stepping on the snow –
Who stands in front with little tapping feet,
And baby-dimpled hands that hide inclosed
Those sleeping crickets, the dark castanets.
But soon the gilded balls have ceased to play
And Annibal is leaping through the hoops,
That turn to twelve, meeting him as he flies
In the swift circle.   Shuddering he leaps,
But with each spring flies swift and swifter still
To loud and louder shouts, while the great hoops
Are changed to smaller. Now the crowd is fired.
The motion swift, the living victim urged,
The imminent failure and repeated scape
Hurry all pulses and intoxicate
With subtle wine of passion many-mixt.

'Tis all about a monkey leaping hard
Till near to gasping ; but it serves as well
As the great circus or arena dire,
Where these are lacking.   Roldan cautiously
Slackens the leaps and lays the hoops to rest,
And Annibal retires with reeling brain
And backward stagger—pity, he could not smile !

Now Roldan spreads his carpet, now he shows
Strange metamorphoses : the pebble black
Changes to whitest egg within his hand ;
A staring rabbit, with retreating ears,
Is swallowed by the air and vanishes ;
He tells men's thoughts about the shaken dice,
Their secret choosings ; makes the white beans
        pass
With causeless act sublime from cup to cup
Turned empty on the ground—diablerie
That pales the girls and puzzles all the boys :
These tricks are samples, hinting to the town
Roldan's great mastery.   He tumbles next,
And Annibal is called to mock each feat
With arduous comicality and save
By rule romantic the great public mind
(And Roldan's body) from too serious strain.

But with the tumbling, lest the feats should fail,
And so need veiling in a haze of sound,
Pablo awakes the viol and the bow—
The masculine bow that draws the woman's
        heart
From out the strings and makes them cry, yearn,
        plead,
Tremble, exult, with mystic union
Of joy acute and tender suffering.
To play the viol and discreetly mix
Alternate with the bow's keen biting tones

The throb responsive to the finger's touch,
Was rarest skill that Pablo half had caught
From an old blind and wandering Catalan ;
The other half was rather heritage
From treasure stored by generations past
In winding chambers of receptive sense.

The wingéd sounds exalt the thick-pressed
    crowd
With a new pulse in common, blending all
The gazing life into one larger soul
With dimly widened consciousness : as waves
In heightened movement tell of waves far off.
And the light changes ; westward stationed
    clouds,
The sun's ranged outposts, luminous message
    spread,
Rousing quiescent things to doff their shade
And show themselves as added audience.
Now Pablo, letting fall the eager bow,
Solicits softer murmurs from the strings,
And now above them pours a wondrous voice
(Such as Greek reapers heard in Sicily)
With wounding rapture in it, like love's arrows ;
And clear upon clear air as colored gems
Dropped in a crystal cup of water pure,
Fall words of sadness, simple, lyrical :

> *Spring comes hither,*
>   *Buds the rose ;*
> *Roses wither,*
>   *Sweet spring goes.*
> *Ojalà, would she carry me !*
>
> *Summer soars—*
>   *Wide-winged day*
> *White light pours,*
>   *Flies away.*
> *Ojalà, would he carry me !*

Soft winds blow,
    Westward born,
Onward go
    Toward the morn.
Ojalà, would they carry me !

Sweet birds sing
    O'er the graves,
Then take wing
    O'er the waves.
Ojalà, would they carry me !

When the voice paused and left the viol's note
To plead forsaken, 'twas as when a cloud
Hiding the sun, makes all the leaves and flowers
Shiver.   But when with measured change the
    strings
Had taught regret new longing, clear again,
Welcome as hope recovered, flowed the voice.

Warm whispering through the slender olive leaves
    Came to me a gentle sound,
    Whispering of a secret found
In the clear sunshine 'mid the golden sheaves :
Said it was sleeping for me in the morn,
    Called it gladness, called it joy,
    Drew me on—" Come hither, boy"—
To where the blue wings rested on the corn.
I thought the gentle sound had whispered true—
    Thought the little heaven mine,
    Leaned to clutch the thing divine,
And saw the blue wings melt within the blue.

The long notes linger on the trembling air,
With subtle penetration enter all
The myriad corridors of the passionate soul,
Message-like spread, and answering action rouse.
Not angular jigs that warm the chilly limbs
In hoary northern mists, but action curved

To soft andante strains pitched plaintively.
Vibrations sympathetic stir all limbs :
Old men live backward in their dancing prime,
And move in memory ; small legs and arms
With pleasant agitation purposeless
Go up and down like pretty fruits in gales.
All long in common for the expressive act
Yet wait for it ; as in the olden time
Men waited for the bard to tell their thought.
"The dance ! the dance !" is shouted all around.
Now Pablo lifts the bow, Pepíta now,
Ready as bird that sees the sprinkled corn,
When Juan nods and smiles, puts forth her foot
And lifts her arm to wake the castanets.
Juan advances, too, from out the ring
And bends to quit his lute ; for now the scene
Is empty ; Roldan weary, gathers pence,
Followed by Annibal with purse and stick.
The carpet lies a colored isle untrod,
Inviting feet : " The dance, the dance," re-
        sounds,
The bow entreats with slow melodic strain,
And all the air with expectation yearns.

Sudden, with gliding motion like a flame
That through dim vapor makes a path of glory,
A figure lithe, all white and saffron-robed,
Flashed right across the circle, and now stood
With ripened arms uplift and regal head,
Like some tall flower whose dark and intense
        heart
Lies half within a tulip-tinted cup.

Juan stood fixed and pale ; Pepíta stepped
Backward within the ring : the voices fell
From shouts insistent to more passive tones
Half meaning welcome, half astonishment.
"Lady Fedalma !—will she dance for us?"

But she, sole swayed by impulse passionate,
Feeling all life was music and all eyes
The warming quickening light that music makes,
Moved as, in dance religious, Miriam,
When on the Red Sea shore she raised her
       voice
And led the chorus of the people's joy;
Or as the Trojan maids that reverent sang
Watching the sorrow-crownéd Hecuba :
Moved in slow curves voluminous, gradual,
Feeling and action flowing into one,
In Eden's natural taintless marriage-bond ;
Ardently modest, sensuously pure,
With young delight that wonders at itself
And throbs as innocent as opening flowers,
Knowing not comment—soilless, beautiful.
The spirit in her gravely glowing face
With sweet community informs her limbs,
Filling their fine gradation with the breath
Of virgin majesty ; as full vowelled words
Are new impregnate with the master's thought.
Even the chance-strayed delicate tendrils black,
That backward 'scape from out her wreathing
       hair—
Even the pliant folds that cling transverse
When with obliquely soaring bend altern
She seems a goddess quitting earth again—
Gather expression—a soft undertone
And resonance exquisite from the grand chord
Of her harmoniously bodied soul.

At first a reverential silence guards
The eager senses of the gazing crowd :
They hold their breath, and live by seeing her.
But soon the admiring tension finds relief—
Sighs of delight, applausive murmurs low,
And stirrings gentle as of earéd corn

Or seed-bent grasses, when the ocean's breath
Spreads landward.   Even Juan is impelled
By the swift-travelling movement: fear and
      doubt
Give way before the hurrying energy ;
He takes his lute and strikes in fellowship,
Filling more full the rill of melody
Raised ever and anon to clearest flood
By Pablo's voice, that dies away too soon,
Like the sweet blackbird's fragmentary chant,
Yet wakes again, with varying rise and fall,
In songs that seem emergent memories
Prompting brief utterance—little canciós
And villancicos, Andalusia-born.

PABLO (*sings*).

It was in the prime
Of the sweet Spring-time.
  In the linnet's throat
  Trembled the love-note,
And the love-stirred air
Thrilled the blossoms there.
  Little shadows danced
    Each a tiny elf,
  Happy in large light
    And the thinnest self.

It was but a minute
  In a far-off Spring,
  But each gentle thing,
Sweetly-wooing linnet,
Soft-thrilled hawthorn tree,
  Happy shadowy elf
  With the thinnest self,
Live still on in me.
O the sweet, sweet prime
Of the past Spring-time !

And still the light is changing : high above
Float soft pink clouds ; others with deeper flush
Stretch like flamingoes bending toward the
    south.
Comes a more solemn brilliance o'er the sky,
A meaning more intense upon the air—
The inspiration of the dying day.
And Juan now, when Pablo's notes subside,
Soothes the regretful ear, and breaks the pause
With masculine voice in deep antiphony.

JUAN (*sings*).

Day is dying !   Float, O song,
   Down the westward river,
Requiem chanting to the Day—
   Day, the mighty Giver.

Pierced by shafts of Time he bleeds,
   Melted rubies sending
Through the river and the sky,
   Earth and heaven blending ;

All the long-drawn earthy banks
   Up to cloud-land lifting :
Slow between them drifts the swan,
   'Twixt two heavens drifting.

Wings half open, like a flow'r
   Inly deeper flushing,
Neck and breast as virgin's pure—
   Virgin proudly blushing.

Day is dying !   Float, O swan,
   Down the ruby river ;
Follow, song, in requiem
   To the mighty Giver.

The exquisite hour, the ardor of the crowd,
The strains more plenteous, and the gathering
        might
Of action passionate where no effort is,
But self's poor gates open to rushing power
That blends the inward ebb and outward vast—
All gathering influences culminate
And urge Fedalma.   Earth and heaven seem one,
Life a glad trembling on the outer edge
Of unknown rapture.   Swifter now she moves,
Filling the measure with a double beat
And widening circle ; now she seems to glow
With more declaréd presence, glorified.
Circling, she lightly bends and lifts on high
The multitudinous-sounding tambourine,
And makes it ring and boom, then lifts it higher,
Stretching her left arm beauteous ; now the
        crowd
Exultant shouts, forgetting poverty
In the rich moment of possessing her.

But sudden, at one point, the exultant throng
Is pushed and hustled, and then thrust apart :
Something approaches—something cuts the ring
Of jubilant idlers—startling as a streak
From alien wounds across the booming flesh
Of careless sporting childhood.   'Tis the band
Of Gypsy prisoners.   Soldiers lead the van
And make sparse flanking guard, aloof surveyed
By gallant Lopez, stringent in command.
The Gypsies chained in couples, all save one,
Walk in dark file with grand bare legs and arms
And savage melancholy in their eyes
That star-like gleam from out black clouds of hair ;
Now they are full in sight, and now they stretch
Right to the centre of the open space.
Fedalma now, with gentle wheeling sweep

Returning, like the loveliest of the Hours
Strayed from her sisters, truant lingering,
Faces again the centre, swings again
The uplifted tambourine. . . .
                    When lo ! with sound
Stupendous throbbing, solemn as a voice
Sent by the invisible choir of all the dead,
Tolls the great passing bell that calls to prayer
For souls departed : at the mighty beat
It seems the light sinks awe-struck—'tis the note
Of the sun's burial ; speech and action pause ;
Religious silence and the holy sign
Of everlasting memories (the sign
Of death that turned to more diffusive life)
Pass o'er the Plaça.   Little children gaze
With lips apart, and feel the unknown god ;
And the most men and women pray.   Not all.
The soldiers pray ; the Gypsies stand unmoved
As pagan statues with proud level gaze.
But he who wears a solitary chain
Heading the file, has turned to face Fedalma.
She motionless, with arm uplifted, guards
The tambourine aloft (lest, sudden-lowered,
Its trivial jingle mar the duteous pause),
Reveres the general prayer, but prays not,
    stands
With level glance meeting that Gypsy's eyes,
That seem to her the sadness of the world
Rebuking her, the great bell's hidden thought
Now first unveiled—the sorrows unredeemed
Of races outcast, scorned, and wandering.
Why does he look at her ? why she at him ?
As if the meeting light between their eyes
Made permanent union ?   His deep-knit brow,
Inflated nostril, scornful lip compressed,
Seem a dark hieroglyph of coming fate
Written before her.   Father Isidor

Had terrible eyes and was her enemy ;
She knew it and defied him ; all her soul
Rounded and hardened in its separateness
When they encountered.   But this prisoner—
This Gypsy, passing, gazing casually—
Was he her enemy too ?   She stood all quelled,
The impetuous joy that hurried in her veins
Seemed backward rushing turned to chillest awe,
Uneasy wonder, and a vague self-doubt.
The minute brief stretched measureless, dream-
       filled
By a dilated new-fraught consciousness.

Now it was gone ; the pious murmur ceased,
The Gypsies all moved onward at command
And careless noises blent confusedly.
But the ring closed again, and many ears
Waited for Pablo's music, many eyes
Turned toward the carpet : it lay bare and dim,
Twilight was there—the bright Fedalma gone.

---

*A handsome room in the Castle.   On a table a
         rich jewel-casket.*

Silva had doffed his mail and with it all
The heavier harness of his warlike cares.
He had not seen Fedalma ; miser-like
He hoarded through the hour a costlier joy
By longing oft-repressed.   Now it was earned ;
And with observance wonted he would send
To ask admission.   Spanish gentlemen
Who wooed fair dames of noble ancestry
Did homage with rich tunics and slashed sleeves
And outward-surging linen's costly snow ;
With broidered scarf transverse, and rosary
Handsomely wrought to fit high-blooded prayer ;
So hinting in how deep respect they held

That self they threw before their lady's feet.
And Silva—that Fedalma's rate should stand
No jot below the highest, that her love
Might seem to all the royal gift it was—
Turned every trifle in his mien and garb
To scrupulous language, uttering to the world
That since she loved him he went carefully,
Bearing a thing so precious in his hand.
A man of high-wrought strain, fastidious
In his acceptance, dreading all delight
That speedy dies and turns to carrion :
His senses much exacting, deep instilled
With keen imagination's airy needs ;—
Like strong-limbed monsters studded o'er with
          eyes,
Their hunger checked by overwhelming vision,
Or that fierce lion in symbolic dream
Snatched from the ground by wings and new-
          endowed
With a man's thought-propelled relenting heart.
Silva was both the lion and the man ;
First hesitating shrank, then fiercely sprang,
Or having sprung, turned pallid at his deed
And loosed the prize, paying his blood for
          nought.
A nature half-transformed, with qualities
That oft bewrayed each other, elements
Not blent but struggling, breeding strange effects,
Passing the reckoning of his friends or foes.
Haughty and generous, grave and passionate ;
With tidal moments of devoutest awe,
Sinking anon to farthest ebb of doubt ;
Deliberating ever, till the sting
Of a recurrent ardor made him rush
Right against reasons that himself had drilled
And marshalled painfully.   A spirit framed
Too proudly special for obedience,

Too subtly pondering for mastery :
Born of a goddess with a mortal sire,
Heir of flesh-fettered, weak divinity,
Doom-gifted with long resonant consciousness
And perilous heightening of the sentient soul.
But look less curiously : life itself
May not express us all, may leave the worst
And the best too, like tunes in mechanism
Never awaked.   In various catalogues
Objects stand variously.   Silva stands
As a young Spaniard, handsome, noble, brave,
With titles many, high in pedigree ;
Or, as a nature quiveringly poised
In reach of storms, whose qualities may turn
To murdered virtues that still walk as ghosts
Within the shuddering soul and shriek remorse ;
Or, as a lover . . . .   In the screening time
Of purple blossoms, when the petals crowd
And softly crush like cherub cheeks in heaven,
Who thinks of greenly withered fruit and
          worms ?
O the warm southern spring is beauteous !
And in love's spring all good seems possible :
No threats, all promise, brooklets ripple full
And bathe the rushes, vicious crawling things
Are pretty eggs, the sun shines graciously
And parches not, the silent rain beats warm
As childhood's kisses, days are young and grow,
And earth seems in its sweet beginning time
Fresh made for two who live in Paradise.
Silva is in love's spring, its freshness breathed
Within his soul along the dusty ways
While marching homeward ; 'tis around him now
As in a garden fenced in for delight,—
And he may seek delight.   Smiling he lifts
A whistle from his belt, but lets it fall
Ere it has reached his lips, jarred by the sound

Of ushers' knocking, and a voice that craves
Admission for the Prior of San Domingo.

PRIOR (*entering*).

You look perturbed, my son. I thrust myself
Between you and some beckoning intent
That wears a face more smiling. than my own.

DON SILVA.

Father, enough that you are here. I wait,
As always, your commands—nay, should have
    sought
An early audience.

PRIOR.

        To give, I trust,
Good reasons for your change of policy?

DON SILVA.

Strong reasons, father.

PRIOR.

             Ay, but are they good?
I have known reasons strong, but strongly evil.

DON SILVA.

'Tis possible. I but deliver mine
To your strict judgment.   Late despatches sent
With urgence by the Count of Bavien,
No hint on my part prompting, with besides
The testified concurrence of the king
And our Grand Master, have made peremptory
The course which else had been but rational.
Without the forces furnished by allies
The siege of Guadix would be madness.   More,
El Zagal has his eyes upon Bedmár :
Let him attempt it : in three weeks from hence
The Master and the Lord of Aguilar
Will bring their forces.   We shall catch the Moors,

The last gleaned clusters of their bravest men,
As in a trap.   You have my reasons, father.

PRIOR.

And they sound well.   But free-tongued rumor
        adds
A pregnant supplement—in substance this :
That inclination snatches arguments
To make indulgence seem judicious choice ;
That you, commanding in God's Holy War,
Lift prayers to Satan to retard the fight
And give you time for feasting—wait a siege,
Call daring enterprise impossible,
Because you'd marry !   You, a Spanish duke,
Christ's general, would marry like a clown,
Who, selling fodder dearer for the war,
Is all the merrier ; nay, like the brutes,
Who know no awe to check their appetite,
Coupling 'mid heaps of slain, while still in front
The battle rages.

DON SILVA.
            Rumor on your lips

Is eloquent, father.

PRIOR.
            Is she true ?

DON SILVA.
                        Perhaps.

I seek to justify my public acts
And not my private joy.   Before the world
Enough if I am faithful in command,
Betray not by my deeds, swerve from no task
My knightly vows constrain me to: herein
I ask all men to test me.

PRIOR.
                    Knightly vows?
Is it by their constraint that you must marry?

DON SILVA.

Marriage is not a breach of them.   I use
A sanctioned liberty . . . . your pardon, father,
I need not teach you what the Church decrees.
But facts may weaken texts, and so dry up
The fount of eloquence.   The Church relaxed
Our Order's rule before I took the vows.

PRIOR.

Ignoble liberty ! you snatch your rule
From what God tolerates, not what he loves ?—
Inquire what lowest offering may suffice,
Cheapen it meanly to an obolus,
Buy, and then count the coin left in your purse
For your debauch ?—Measure obedience
By scantest powers of brethren whose frail flesh
Our Holy Church indulges ?—Ask great Law,
The rightful Sovereign of the human soul,
For what it pardons, not what it commands ?
O fallen knighthood, penitent of high vows,
Asking a charter to degrade itself !
Such poor apology of rules relaxed
Blunts not suspicion of that doubleness
Your enemies tax you with.

DON SILVA.

                   Oh, for the rest,
Conscience is harder than our enemies,
Knows more, accuses with more nicety,
Nor needs to question Rumor if we fall
Below the perfect model of our thought.
I fear no outward arbiter.—You smile ?

PRIOR.

Ay, at the contrast 'twixt your portraiture
And the true image of your conscience, shown
As now I see it in your acts.   I see
A drunken sentinel who gives alarm

At his own shadow, but when scalers snatch
His weapon from his hand smiles idiot-like
At games he's dreaming of.

DON SILVA.

                A parable !
The husk is rough—holds something bitter,
    doubtless.

PRIOR.

Oh, the husk gapes with meaning over-ripe.
You boast a conscience that controls your deeds,
Watches your knightly armor, guards your rank
From stain of treachery—you, helpless slave,
Whose will lies nerveless in the clutch of lust—
Of blind mad passion—passion itself most help-
    less,
Storm-driven, like the monsters of the sea.
O famous conscience !

DON SILVA.

              Pause there ! Leave unsaid
Aught that will match that text.   More were too
    much,
Even from holy lips.   I own no love
But such as guards my honor, since it guards
Hers whom I love !   I suffer no foul words
To stain the gift I lay before her feet ;
And, being hers, my honor is more safe.

PRIOR.

Versemakers' talk ! fit for a world of rhymes,
Where facts are feigned to tickle idle ears,
Where good and evil play at tournament
And end in amity—a world of lies—
A carnival of words where every year
Stale falsehoods serve fresh men.   Your honor
    safe ?

What honor has a man with double bonds?
Honor is shifting as the shadows are
To souls that turn their passions into laws.
A Christian knight who weds an infidel . . . .

> DON SILVA (*fiercely*).

An infidel!

> PRIOR.

       May one day spurn the Cross,
And call that honor!—one day find his sword
Stained with his brother's blood, and call that
    honor!
Apostates' honor?—harlots' chastity!
Renegades' faithfulness?—Iscariot's!

> DON SILVA.

Strong words and burning; but they scorch not
    me.
Fedalma is a daughter of the Church—
Has been baptized and nurtured in the faith.

> PRIOR.

Ay, as a thousand Jewesses, who yet
Are brides of Satan in a robe of flames.

> DON SILVA.

Fedalma is no Jewess, bears no marks
That tell of Hebrew blood.

> PRIOR.

          She bears the marks
Of races unbaptized, that never bowed
Before the holy signs, were never moved
By stirrings of the sacramental gifts.

> DON SILVA (*scornfully*).

Holy accusers practise palmistry,
And, other witness lacking, read the skin.

PRIOR.

I read a record deeper than the skin.
What ! Shall the trick of nostrils and of lips
Descend through generations, and the soul
That moves within our frame like God in worlds—
Convulsing, urging, melting, withering—
Imprint no record, leave no documents,
Of her great history ? Shall men bequeath
The fancies of their palate to their sons,
And shall the shudder of restraining awe,
The slow-wept tears of contrite memory,
Faith's prayerful labor, and the food divine
Of fasts ecstatic—shall these pass away
Like wind upon the waters, tracklessly ?
Shall the mere curl of eyelashes remain,
And god-enshrining symbols leave no trace
Of tremors reverent ?—That maiden's blood
Is as unchristian as the leopard's.

DON SILVA.

                                    Say,
Unchristian as the Blessed Virgin's blood
Before the angel spoke the word, " All hail !"

PRIOR (*smiling bitterly*).

Said I not truly ? See, your passion weaves
Already blasphemies !

DON SILVA.

                        'Tis you provoke them.

PRIOR.

I strive, as still the Holy Spirit strives,
To move the will perverse. But, failing this,
God commands other means to save our blood,
To save Castilian glory—nay, to save
The name of Christ from blot of traitorous
    deeds.

DON SILVA.

Of traitorous deeds! Age, kindred, and your
    cowl,
Give an ignoble license to your tongue.
As for your threats, fulfil them at your peril.
'Tis you, not I, will gibbet our great name
To rot in infamy. If I am strong
In patience now, trust me, I can be strong
Then in defiance.

PRIOR.

    Miserable man !
Your strength will turn to anguish, like the
    strength
Of fallen angels. Can you change your blood ?
You are a Christian, with the Christian awe
In every vein. A Spanish noble, born
To serve your people and your people's faith.
Strong, are you ? Turn your back upon the
    Cross—
Its shadow is before you. Leave your place :
Quit the great ranks of knighthood : you will walk
Forever with a tortured double self,
A self that will be hungry while you feast,
Will blush with shame while you are glorified,
Will feel the ache and chill of desolation.
Even in the very bosom of your love.
Mate yourself with this woman, fit for what ?
To make the sport of Moorish palaces,
A lewd Herodias . . . .

DON SILVA.

        Stop ! no other man,
Priest though he were, had had his throat left
    free
For passage of those words. I would have
    clutched

His serpent's neck, and flung him out to hell !
A monk must needs defile the name of love :
He knows it but as tempting devils paint it.
You think to scare my love from its resolve
With arbitrary consequences, strained
By rancorous effort from the thinnest motes
Of possibility ?—cite hideous lists
Of sins irrelevant, to frighten me
With bugbears' names, as women fright a child?
Poor pallid wisdom, taught by inference
From blood-drained life, where phantom terrors
    rule,
And all achievement is to leave undone !
Paint the day dark, make sunshine cold to me,
Abolish the earth's fairness, prove it all
A fiction of my eyes—then, after that,
Profane Fedalma.

           PRIOR.

        O there is no need :
She has profaned herself.   Go, raving man,
And see her dancing now.   Go, see your bride
Flaunting her beauties grossly in the gaze
Of vulgar idlers—eking out the show
Made in the Plaça by a mountebank.
I hinder you no farther.

          DON SILVA.

         It is false !

          PRIOR.

Go, prove it false, then.

         [Father Isidor
Drew on his cowl and turned away.   The face
That flashed anathemas, in swift eclipse
Seemed Silva's vanished confidence.   In haste
He rushed unsignalled through the corridor

To where the Duchess once, Fedalma now,
Had residence retired from din of arms—
Knocked, opened, found all empty—said
With muffled voice, " Fedalma !"—called more
  loud,
More oft on Iñez, the old trusted nurse—
Then searched the terrace-garden, calling still,
But heard no answering sound, and saw no face
Save painted faces staring all unmoved
By agitated tones. He hurried back,
Giving half-conscious orders as he went
To page and usher, that they straight should seek
Lady Fedalma ; then with stinging shame
Wished himself silent ; reached again the room
Where still the Father's menace seemed to hang
Thickening the air ; snatched cloak and pluméd
  hat,
And grasped, not knowing why, his poniard's
  hilt ;
Then checked himself and said :—]

                        If he spoke truth !
To know were wound enough—to see the truth
Were fire upon the wound. It must be false !
His hatred saw amiss, or snatched mistake
In other men's report. I am a fool !
But where can she be gone ? gone secretly ?
And in my absence? Oh, she meant no wrong !
I am a fool !—But where can she be gone ?
With only Iñez? Oh, she meant no wrong !
I swear she never meant it. There's no wrong
But she would make it momentary right
By innocence in doing it. . . .
                        And yet,
What is our certainty ? Why, knowing all
That is not secret. Mighty confidence !
One pulse of Time makes the base hollow—sends

The towering certainty we built so high
Toppling in fragments meaningless.   What is—
What will be—must be—pooh ! they wait the key
Of that which is not yet ; all other keys
Are made of our conjectures, take their sense
From humors fooled by hope, or by despair.
Know what is good ?   O God, we know not yet
If bliss itself is not young misery
With fangs swift growing. . . .
                              But some outward harm
May even now be hurting, grieving her.
Oh ! I must search—face shame—if shame be
        there.
Here, Perez ! hasten to Don Alvar—tell him
Lady Fedalma must be sought—is lost—
Has met, I fear, some mischance. He must send
Toward divers points.   I go myself to seek
First in the town. . . .

                              [As Perez oped the door,
Then moved aside for passage of the Duke,
Fedalma entered, cast away the cloud
Of serge and linen, and outbeaming bright,
Advanced a pace toward Silva—but then paused,
For he had started and retreated ; she,
Quick and responsive as the subtle air
To change in him, divined that she must wait
Until they were alone : they stood and looked.
Within the Duke was struggling confluence
Of feelings manifold—pride, anger, dread,
Meeting in stormy rush with sense secure
That she was present, with the new-stilled thirst
Of gazing love, with trust inevitable
As in beneficent virtues of the light
And all earth's sweetness, that Fedalma's soul
Was free from blemishing purpose.   Yet proud
        wrath

Leaped in dark flood above the purer stream
That strove to drown it : Anger seeks its prey—
Something to tear with sharp-edged tooth and
    claw,
Likes not to go off hungry, leaving Love
To feast on milk and honeycomb at will.
Silva's heart said, he must be happy soon,
She being there ; but to be happy—first
He must be angry, having cause.   Yet love
Shot like a stifled cry of tenderness
All through the harshness he would fain have
    given
To the dear word,]

DON SILVA.

Fedalma !

FEDALMA.

            O my lord !
You are come back, and I was wandering !

DON SILVA (*coldly but with suppressed agitation*).

You meant I should be ignorant.

FEDALMA.

            Oh no,
I should have told you after—not before,
Lest you should hinder me.

DON SILVA.

         Then my known wish
Can make no hindrance?

FEDALMA (*archly*).

          That depends
On what the wish may be.   You wished me once
Not to uncage the birds.   I meant to obey :
But in a moment something—something stronger,

Forced me to let them out.   It did no harm.
They all came back again—the silly birds !
I told you, after.

      DON SILVA (*with haughty coldness*).
             Will you tell me now
What was the prompting stronger than my wish
That made you wander ?

FEDALMA (*advancing a step toward him, with a
        sudden look of anxiety*).
             Are you angry ?

      DON SILVA (*smiling bitterly*).
                     Angry ?
A man deep-wounded may feel too much pain
To feel much anger.

      FEDALMA (*still more anxiously*).
             You—deep-wounded ?

      DON SILVA.
                          Yes !

Have I not made your place and dignity
The very heart of my ambition ?   You—
No enemy could do it—you alone
Can strike it mortally.

        FEDALMA.
           Nay, Silva, nay.
Has some one told you false ?   I only went
To see the world with Iñez—see the town,
The people, everything.   It was no harm.
I did not mean to dance : it happened so
At last . . .
        DON SILVA.
        O God, it's true then !—true that you,
A maiden nurtured as rare flowers are,
The very air of heaven sifted fine

Lest any mote should mar your purity,
Have flung yourself out on the dusty way
For common eyes to see your beauty soiled !
You own it true—you danced upon the Plaça ?

FEDALMA (*proudly*).

Yes, it is true.   I was not wrong to dance.
The air was filled with music, with a song
That seemed the voice of the sweet eventide—
The glowing light entering through eye and ear—
That seemed our love—mine, yours—they are
      but one—
Trembling through all my limbs, as fervent words
Tremble within my soul and must be spoken.
And all the people felt a common joy
And shouted for the dance.   A brightness soft
As of the angels moving down to see
Illumined the broad space.   The joy, the life
Around, within me, were one heaven : I longed
To blend them visibly : I longed to dance
Before the people—be as mounting flame
To all that burned within them ! Nay, I danced ;
There was no longing : I but did the deed
Being moved to do it.

(*As* FEDALMA *speaks, she and* DON SILVA *are
    gradually drawn nearer to each other.*)

               Oh ! I seemed new-waked
To life in unison with a multitude—
Feeling my soul upborne by all their souls,
Floating within their gladness !   Soon I lost
All sense of separateness : Fedalma died
As a star dies, and melts into the light.
I was not, but joy was, and love and triumph.
Nay, my dear lord, I never could do aught
But I must feel you present.   And once done,

Why, you must love it better than your wish.
I pray you, say so—say, it was not wrong !

(*While* FEDALMA *has been making this last appeal, they have gradually come close together,
and at last embrace.*)

DON SILVA (*holding her hands*).

Dangerous rebel ! if the world without
Were pure as that within . . . but 'tis a book
Wherein you only read the poesy
And miss all wicked meanings.   Hence the need
For trust—obedience—call it what you will—
Toward him whose life will be your guard—
          toward me
Who now am soon to be your husband.

FEDALMA.
                                        Yes !
That very thing that when I am your wife
I shall be something different,—shall be
I know not what, a Duchess with new thoughts—
For nobles never think like common men,
Nor wives like maidens (Oh, you wot not yet
How much I note, with all my ignorance)—
That very thing has made me more resolve
To have my will before I am your wife.
How can the Duchess ever satisfy
Fedalma's unwed eyes? and so to-day
I scolded Iñez till she cried and went.

DON SILVA.

It was a guilty weakness : she knows well
That since you pleaded to be left more free
From tedious tendance and control of dames
Whose rank matched better with your destiny,
Her charge—my trust—was weightier.

FEDALMA.

Nay, my lord,
You must not blame her, dear old nurse. She
    cried.
Why, you would have consented too, at last
I said such things ! I was resolved to go,
And see the streets, the shops, the men at work.
The women, little children—everything,
Just as it is when nobody looks on.
And I have done it ! We were out four hours.
I feel so wise.

DON SILVA.

Had you but seen the town,
You innocent naughtiness, not shown yourself—
Shown yourself dancing—you bewilder me !—
Frustrate my judgment with strange negatives
That seem like poverty, and yet are wealth
In precious womanliness, beyond the dower
Of other women : wealth in virgin gold,
Outweighing all their petty currency.
You daring modesty ! You shrink no more
From gazing men than from the gazing flowers
That, dreaming sunshine, open as you pass.

FEDALMA.

No, I should like the world to look at me
With eyes of love that make a second day.
I think your eyes would keep the life in me
Though I had nought to feed on else.   Their blue
Is better than the heavens'—holds more love
For me, Fedalma—is a little heaven
For this one little world that looks up now.

DON SILVA.

O precious little world ! you make the heaven
As the earth makes the sky.   But, dear, all eyes

Though looking even on you, have not a glance
That cherishes . . . .

FEDALMA.

   Ah no, I meant to tell you—
Tell how my dancing ended with a pang.
There came a man, one among many more,
But *he* came first, with iron on his limbs.
And when the bell tolled, and the people prayed,
And I stood pausing—then he looked at me.
O Silva, such a man !   I thought he rose
From the dark place of long-imprisoned souls,
To say that Christ had never come to them.
It was a look to shame a seraph's joy.
And make him sad in heaven. It found me there—
Seemed to have travelled far to find me there
And grasp me—claim this festal life of mine
As heritage of sorrow, chill my blood
With the cold iron of some unknown bonds.
The gladness hurrying full within my veins
Was sudden frozen, and I danced no more.
But seeing you let loose the stream of joy,
Mingling the present with the sweetest past.
Yet, Silva, still I see him.   Who is he?
Who are those prisoners with him ?   Are they
  Moors ?

DON SILVA.

No, they are Gypsies, strong and cunning knaves,
A double game to us by the Moors' loss :
The man you mean—their chief—is an ally
The infidel will miss.   His look might chase
A herd of monks, and make them fly more swift
Than from St. Jerome's lion.   Such vague fear,
Such bird-like tremors when that savage glance
Turned full upon you in your height of joy
Was natural, was not worth emphasis.
Forget it, dear,   This hour is worth whole days

When we are sundered.   Danger urges us
To quick resolve.

FEDALMA.

What danger ? what resolve ?
I never felt chill shadow in my heart
Until this sunset.

DON SILVA.

A dark enmity
Plots how to sever us.   And our defence
Is speedy marriage, secretly achieved,
Then publicly declared.   Beseech you, dear,
Grant me this confidence ; do my will in this,
Trusting the reasons why I overset
All my own airy building raised so high
Of bridal honors, marking when you step
From off your maiden throne to come to me
And bear the yoke of love.   There is great need.
I hastened home, carrying this prayer to you
Within my heart.   The bishop is my friend,
Furthers our marriage, holds in enmity—
Some whom we love not and who love not us.
By this night's moon our priest will be despatched
From Jaën.   I shall march an escort strong
To meet him.   Ere a second sun from this
Has risen—you consenting—we may wed.

FEDALMA.

None knowing that we wed ?

DON SILVA.

Beforehand none
Save Iñez and Don Alvar.   But the vows
Once safely binding us, my household all
Shall know you as their Duchess.   No man
        then
Can aim a blow at you but through my breast,

And what stains you must stain our ancient
        name ;
If any hate you I will take his hate,
And wear it as a glove upon my helm ;
Nay, God himself will never have the power
To strike you solely and leave me unhurt,
He having made us one.   Now put the seal
Of your dear lips on that.

FEDALMA.

               A solemn kiss ?—
Such as I gave you when you came that day
From Córdova, when first we said we loved ?
When you had left the ladies of the Court
For thirst to see me ; and you told me so,
And then I seemed to know why I had lived.
I never knew before.   A kiss like that ?

DON SILVA.

Yes, yes, you face divine ! When was our
        kiss
Like any other ?

FEDALMA.

          Nay, I cannot tell
What other kisses are. But that one kiss
Remains upon my lips. The angels, spirits,
Creatures with finer sense, may see it there.
And now another kiss that will not die,
Saying, To-morrow I shall be your wife !

        (*They kiss, and pause a moment, looking
           earnestly in each other's eyes. Then*
           FEDALMA, *breaking away from* DON
           SILVA, *stands at a little distance from
           him with a look of roguish delight.*)

Now I am glad I saw the town to-day
Before I am a Duchess—glad I gave

This poor Fedalma all her wish.   For once,
Long years ago, I cried when Iñez said,
" You are no more a little girl ;" I grieved
To part for ever from that little girl
And all her happy world so near the ground.
It must be sad to outlive aught we love.
So I shall grieve a little for these days
Of poor unwed Fedalma.   Oh, they are sweet,
And none will come just like them.   Perhaps the
     wind
Wails so in winter for the summers dead,
And all sad sounds are nature's funeral cries
For   what   has   been   and   is   not.   Are   they,
     Silva ?

> (*She comes nearer to him again, and lays
> her hand on his arm, looking up at him
> with melancholy.*)

DON SILVA.

Why, dearest, you began in merriment,
And end as sadly as a widowed bird.
Some touch mysterious has new-tuned your soul
To melancholy sequence.   You soared high
In that wild flight of rapture when you danced,
And now you droop.   'Tis arbitrary grief,
Surfeit of happiness, that mourns for loss
Of unwed love, which does but die like seed
For fuller harvest of our tenderness.
We in our wedded life shall know no loss.
We shall new-date our years.   What went before
Will be the time of promise, shadows, dreams ;
But this, full revelation of great love.
For rivers blent take in a broader heaven,
And we shall blend our souls.   Away with grief !
When   this   dear   head   shall   wear   the   double
     crown

Of wife and Duchess—spiritually crowned
With sworn espousal before God and man—
Visibly crowned with jewels that bespeak
The chosen sharer of my heritage—
My love will gather perfectness, as thoughts
That nourish us to magnanimity
Grow perfect with more perfect utterance,
Gathering full-shapen strength.   And then these
    gems,

      (Don Silva *draws* Fedalma *toward the*
        jewel-casket on the table, and opens it.)

Helping the utterance of my soul's full choice,
Will be the words made richer by just use,
And have new meaning in their lustrousness.
You know these jewels ; they are precious signs
Of long-transmitted honor, heightened still
By worthy wearing ; and I give them you—
Ask you to take them—place our house's trust
In her sure keeping whom my heart has found
Worthiest, most beauteous.   These rubies—
    see—
Were falsely placed if not upon your brow.

      (Fedalma, *while* Don Silva *holds open*
        the casket, bends over it, looking at the
        jewels with delight.)

FEDALMA.

Ah, I remember them.   In childish days
I felt as if they were alive and breathed.
I used to sit with awe and look at them.
And now they will be mine !   I'll put them on.
Help me, my lord, and you shall see me now
Somewhat as I shall look at Court with you,
That we may know if I shall bear them well.
I have a fear sometimes : I think your love

Has never paused within your eyes to look,
And only passes through them into mine.
But when the Court is looking, and the queen,
Your eyes will follow theirs.   Oh, if you saw
That I was other than you wished—'twere death !

DON SILVA (*taking up a jewel and placing it
against her ear*).

Nay, let us try.   Take out your ear-ring, sweet.
This ruby glows with longing for your ear.

FEDALMA (*taking out her ear-rings, and then
lifting up the other jewels, one by one*).
Pray, fasten in the rubies.

(DON SILVA *begins to put in the ear-ring.*)
          I was right !
These gems have life in them : their colors
    speak,
Say what words fail of.   So do many things—
The scent of jasmine, and the fountain's plash,
The moving shadows on the far-off hills,
The slanting moonlight, and our clasping hands.
O Silva, there's an ocean round our words
That overflows and drowns them.   Do you know
Sometimes when we sit silent, and the air
Breathes gently on us from the orange-trees,
It seems that with the whisper of a word
Our souls must shrink, get poorer, more apart.
Is it not true ?
         DON SILVA.

         Yes, dearest, it is true.
Speech is but broken light upon the depth
Of the unspoken : even your loved words
Float in the larger meaning of your voice
As something dimmer.

(*He is still trying in vain to fasten the second ear-ring, while she has stooped again over the casket.*)

FEDALMA (*raising her head*).

     Ah ! your lordly hands
Will never fix that jewel. Let me try.
Women's small finger-tips have eyes.

DON SILVA.

        No, no !
I like the task, only you must be still.

(*She stands perfectly still, clasping her hands together while he fastens the second ear-ring. Suddenly a clanking noise is heard without.*)

FEDALMA (*starting with an expression of pain*).
What is that sound ?—that jarring cruel sound ?
'Tis there—outside.

(*She tries to start away toward the window, but* DON SILVA *detains her.*)

DON SILVA.

     O heed it not, it comes
From workmen in the outer gallery.

FEDALMA.
It is the sound of fetters ; sound of work
Is not so dismal. Hark, they pass along !
I know it is those Gypsy prisoners.
I saw them, heard their chains. O horrible,
To be in chains ! Why, I with all my bliss
Have longed sometimes to fly and be at large ;
Have felt imprisoned in my luxury
With servants for my jailers. O my lord,
Do you not wish the world were different ?

DON SILVA.

It will be different when this war has ceased.
You, wedding me, will make it different,
Making one life more perfect.

FEDALMA.

That is true !
And I shall beg much kindness at your hands
For those who are less happy than ourselves.—
(*Brightening*) Oh I shall rule you ! ask for many
      things
Before the world, which you will not deny
For very pride, lest men should say, '' The Duke
Holds lightly by his Duchess ; he repents
His humble choice.''

> (*She breaks away from him and returns to the
> jewels, taking up a necklace, and clasping
> it on her neck, while he takes a circlet of
> diamonds and rubies and raises it toward
> her head as he speaks.*)

DON SILVA.

Doubtless, I shall persist
In loving you, to disappoint the world ;
Out of pure obstinacy feel myself
Happiest of men.   Now, take the coronet.

> (*He places the circlet on her head.*)

The diamonds want more light.   See, from this
      lamp
I can set tapers burning.

FEDALMA.

Tell me, now,
When all these cruel wars are at an end,
And when we go to Court at Córdova,

Or Seville, or Toledo—wait awhile,
I must be farther off for you to see—

> (*She retreats to a distance from him, and then
> advances slowly.*)

Now think (I would the tapers gave more light !)
If when you show me at the tournaments
Among the other ladies, they will say,
"Duke Silva is well matched.   His bride was
        nought,
Was some poor foster-child, no man knows what ;
Yet is her carriage noble, all her robes
Are worn with grace : she might have been well
        born."
Will they say so ?   Think now we are at Court,
And all eyes bent on me.

Don Silva.

            Fear not, my Duchess !
Some knight who loves may say his lady-love
Is fairer, being fairest.   None can say
Don Silva's bride might better fit her rank.
You will make rank seem natural as kind,
As eagle's plumage or the lion's might.
A crown upon your brow would seem God-made.

Fedalma.

Then I am glad !   I shall try on to-night
The other jewels—have the tapers lit,
And see the diamonds sparkle.

> (*She goes to the casket again.*)
               Here is gold—
A necklace of pure gold—most finely wrought.

> (*She takes out a large gold necklace and holds it
> up before her, then turns to* Don Silva.)

But this is one that you have worn, my lord ?

DON SILVA.

No, love, I never wore it.   Lay it down.

(*He puts the necklace gently out of her hand,
then joins both her hands and holds them
up between his own.*)

You must not look at jewels any more,
But look at me.

FEDALMA (*looking up at him.*)

O you dear heaven !

I should see nought if you were gone.   'Tis true
My mind is too much given to gauds—to things
That fetter thought within this narrow space.
That comes of fear.

DON SILVA.

What fear ?

FEDALMA.

Fear of myself.

For when I walk upon the battlements
And see the river travelling toward the plain,
The mountains screening all the world beyond,
A longing comes that haunts me in my dreams—
Dreams where I seem to spring from off the
    walls,
And fly far, far away, until at last
I find myself alone among the rocks,
Remember then that I have left you—try
To fly back to you—and my wings are gone !

DON SILVA.

A wicked dream !   If ever I left you,
Even in dreams, it was some demon dragged me,
And with fierce struggles I awaked myself.

FEDALMA.

It is a hateful dream, and when it comes—
I mean, when in my waking hours there comes
That longing to be free, I am afraid :
I run down to my chamber, plait my hair,
Weave colors in it, lay out all my gauds,
And in my mind make new ones prettier.
You see I have two minds, and both are foolish.
Sometimes a torrent rushing through my soul
Escapes in wild strange wishes ; presently,
It dwindles to a little babbling rill
And plays among the pebbles and the flowers.
Iñez will have it I lack broidery,
Says nought else gives content to noble maids.
But I have never broidered—never will.
No, when I am a Duchess and a wife
I shall ride forth—may I not ?—by your side.

DON SILVA.

Yes, you shall ride upon a palfrey, black
To match Bavieca.   Not Queen Isabel
Will be a sight more gladdening to men's eyes
Than my dark queen Fedalma.

FEDALMA.

                    Ah, but you,
You are my king, and I shall tremble still
With some great fear that throbs within my love.
Does your love fear ?

DON SILVA.

                Ah, yes ! all preciousness
To mortal hearts is guarded by a fear.
All love fears loss, and most that loss supreme,
Its own perfection—seeing, feeling change
From high to lower, dearer to less dear.
Can love be careless ?   If we lost our love

What should we find ?—with this sweet Past torn
    off,
Our lives deep scarred just where their beauty
    lay?
The best we found thenceforth were still a worse:
The only better is a Past that lives
On through an added Present, stretching still
In hope unchecked by shaming memories
To life's last breath.   And so I tremble too
Before my queen Fedalma.

FEDALMA.

                That is just.
'Twere hard of Love to make us women fear
And leave you bold.   Yet Love is not quite even.
For feeble creatures, little birds and fawns,
Are shaken more by fear, while large strong
    things
Can bear it stoutly. So we women still
Are not well dealt with.   Yet I'd choose to be
Fedalma loving Silva. You, my lord,
Hold the worse share, since you must love poor
    me.
But is it what we love, or how we love,
That makes true good?

DON SILVA.

             O subtlety! for me
'Tis what I love determines how I love.
The goddess with pure rites reveals herself
And makes pure worship.

FEDALMA.

              Do you worship me?

DON SILVA.

Ay, with that best of worship which adores
Goodness adorable.

FEDALMA (*archly*).

          Goodness obedient,
Doing your will, devoutest worshipper?

DON SILVA.

Yes—listening to this prayer.   This very night
I shall go forth.   And you will rise with day
And wait for me?

FEDALMA.

    Yes.

DON SILVA.

            I shall surely come.
And then we shall be married.   Now I go
To audience fixed in Abderahman's tower.
Farewell, love!

                  (*They embrace.*)

FEDALMA.

    Some chill dread possesses me!

DON SILVA.

Oh, confidence has oft been evil augury,
So dread may hold a promise.   Sweet, farewell!
I shall send tendance as I pass, to bear
This casket to your chamber.—One more kiss.

                  (*Exit.*)

FEDALMA (*when* DON SILVA *is gone, returning to
the casket, and looking dreamily at the jewels*).

Yes, now that good seems less impossible!
Now it seems true that I shall be his wife,
Be ever by his side, and make a part
In all his purposes. . . . .
These rubies greet me Duchess.   How they
      glow!
Their prisoned souls are throbbing like my own.

Perchance they loved once, were ambitious,
    proud ;
Or do they only dream of wider life,
Ache from intenseness, yearn to burst the wall
Compact of crystal splendor, and to flood
Some wider space with glory ?   Poor, poor gems !
We must be patient in our prison-house,
And find our space in loving.   Pray you, love
    me.
Let us be glad together.   And you, gold—

        (She takes up the gold necklace.)

You wondrous necklace—will you love me too,
And be my amulet to keep me safe
From eyes that hurt ?

        (She spreads out the necklace, meaning to
          clasp it on her neck.   Then pauses,
          startled, holding it before her.)

                Why, it is magical !
He says he never wore it—yet these lines—
Nay, if he had, I should remember well
'Twas he, no other.   And these twisted lines—
They seem to speak to me as writing would,
To bring a message from the dead, dead past.
What is their secret ?   Are they characters ?
I never learned them ; yet they stir some sense
That once I dreamed—I have forgotten what.
Or was it life ?   Perhaps I lived before
In some strange world where first my soul was
    shaped,
And all this passionate love, and joy, and pain,
That come, I know not whence, and sway my
    deeds,
Are old imperious memories, blind yet strong,
That this world stirs within me ; as this chain
Stirs some strange certainty of visions gone,

And all my mind is as an eye that stares
Into the darkness painfully.

(*While* FEDALMA *has been looking at the necklace,*
    JUAN *has entered, and finding himself un-*
    observed by her, says at last,)

Señora !

FEDALMA *starts, and gathering the necklace to-*
    gether, turns round.

Oh, Juan, it is you !

JUAN.

I met the Duke—
Had waited long without, no matter why—
And when he ordered one to wait on you
And carry forth a burthen you would give,
I prayed for leave to be the servitor.
Don Silva owes me twenty granted wishes
That I have never tendered, lacking aught
That I could wish for and a Duke could grant ;
But this one wish to serve you weighs as much
As twenty other longings.

FEDALMA (*smiling*).

That sounds well.
You turn your speeches prettily as songs.
But I will not forget the many days
You have neglected me.   Your pupil learns
But little from you now.   Her studies flag.
The Duke says, " That is idle Juan's way :
Poets must rove—are honey-sucking birds
And know not constancy."   Said he quite true ?

JUAN.

O lady, constancy has kind and rank.
One man's is lordly, plump and bravely clad,
Holds its head high, and tells the world its name :

Another man's is beggared, must go bare,
And shiver through the world, the jest of all,
But that it puts the motley on, and plays
Itself the jester.   But I see you hold
The Gypsy's necklace : it is quaintly wrought.

FEDALMA.

The Gypsy's ?   Do you know its history ?

JUAN.

No farther back than when I saw it taken
From off its wearer's neck—the Gypsy chief's.

FEDALMA (*eagerly*).

What ! he who paused, at tolling of the bell,
Before me in the Plaça ?

JUAN.

    Yes, I saw
His look fixed on you.

FEDALMA.

   Know you aught of him ?

JUAN.

Something and nothing—as I know the sky,
Or some great story of the olden time
That hides a secret.   I have oft talked with him.
He seems to say much, yet is but a wizard
Who draws down rain by sprinkling ; throws me
  out
Some pregnant text that urges comment ; casts
A sharp-hooked question, baited with such skill
It needs must catch the answer.

FEDALMA.

     It is hard
That such a man should be a prisoner—
Be chained to work.

JUAN.

           Oh, he is dangerous!
Granáda with this Zarca for a king
Might still maim Christendom.   He is of those
Who steal the keys from snoring Destiny
And make the prophets lie.   A Gypsy, too,
Suckled by hunted beasts, whose mother-milk
Has filled his veins with hate.

FEDALMA.

                 I thought his eyes
Spoke not of hatred—seemed to say he bore
The pain of those who never could be saved.
What if the Gypsies are but savage beasts
And must be hunted?—let them be set free,
Have benefit of chase, or stand at bay
And fight for life and offspring.   Prisoners!
Oh! they have made their fires beside the
       streams,
Their walls have been the rocks, the pillared
       pines,
Their roof the living sky that breathes with light:
They may well hate a cage, like strong-winged
       birds,
Like me, who have no wings, but only wishes.
I will beseech the Duke to set them free.

JUAN.

Pardon me, lady, if I seem to warn,
Or try to play the sage.   What if the Duke
Love not to hear of Gypsies? if their name
Were poisoned for him once, being used amiss?
I speak not as of fact.   Our nimble souls
Can spin an insubstantial universe
Suiting our mood, and call it possible,
Sooner than see one grain with eye exact
And give strict record of it.   Yet by chance

Our fancies may be truth and make us seers.
'Tis a rare teeming world, so harvest-full,
Even guessing ignorance may pluck some fruit.
Note what I say no farther than will stead
The siege you lay.   I would not seem to tell
Aught that the Duke may think and yet withhold :
It were a trespass in me.

FEDALMA.

Fear not, Juan.
Your words bring daylight with them when you
        speak.
I understand your care.   But I am brave—
Oh ! and so cunning !—always I prevail.
Now, honored Troubadour, if you will be
Your pupil's servant, bear this casket hence.
Nay, not the necklace : it is hard to place.
Pray go before me ; Iñez will be there.

(*Exit* JUAN *with the casket*).

FEDALMA (*looking again at the necklace*).

It is *his* past clings to you, not my own.
If we have each our angels, good and bad,
Fates, separate from ourselves, who act for us
When we are blind, or sleep, then this man's fate,
Hovering about the thing he used to wear,
Has laid its grasp on mine appealingly.
Dangerous, is he ?—well, a Spanish knight
Would have his enemy strong—defy, not bind
        him.
I can dare all things when my soul is moved
By something hidden that possesses me.
If Silva said this man must keep his chains
I should find ways to free him—disobey
And free him as I did the birds.   But no !
As soon as we are wed, I'll put my prayer,

And he will not deny me : he is good.
Oh, I shall have much power as well as joy !
Duchess Fedalma may do what she will.

———

*A Street by the Castle.   JUAN leans against a
parapet, in moonlight, and touches his lute half
unconsciously.   PEPITA stands on tiptoe watching him, and then advances till her shadow
falls in front of him.   He looks toward her.
A piece of white drapery thrown over her head
catches the moonlight.*

JUAN.

Ha ! my Pepíta ! see how thin and long
Your shadow is.   'Tis so your ghost will be
When you are dead.

PEPITA (*crossing herself*).

Dead !—O the blessed saints !
You would be glad, then, if Pepíta died ?

JUAN.

Glad ! why ?   Dead maidens are not merry.
      Ghosts
Are doleful company.   I like you living.

PEPITA.

I think you like me not.   I wish you did.
Sometimes you sing to me and make me dance ;
Another time you take no heed of me,
Not though I kiss my hand to you and smile.
But Andrès would be glad if I kissed *him.*

JUAN.

My poor Pepíta, I am old.

PEPITA.

No, no.

You have no wrinkles.

JUAN.

        Yes, I have—within ;
The wrinkles are within, my little bird.
Why, I have lived through twice a thousand
    years,
And kept the company of men whose bones
Crumbled before the blessed Virgin lived.

PEPITA (*crossing herself*).
Nay, God defend us, that is wicked talk !
You say it but to scorn me. (*With a sob*) I will
    go.
JUAN.
Stay, little pigeon. I am not unkind.
Come, sit upon the wall. Nay, never cry.
Give me your cheek to kiss. There, cry no more !

(PEPITA, *sitting on the low parapet, puts up her
    cheek to* JUAN, *who kisses it, putting his
    hand under her chin. She takes his hand
    and kisses it.*)

PEPITA.
I like to kiss your hand. It is so good—
So smooth and soft.

JUAN.
    Well, well, I'll sing to you.

PEPITA.
A pretty song, loving and merry ?

JUAN.
        Yes.

(JUAN *sings.*)

Memory,
Tell to me
What is fair,
Past compare,
*   In the land of Tubal?*

Is it Spring's
Lovely things,
Blossoms white,
Rosy dight?
*   Then it is Pepíta.*

Summer's crest
Red-gold tressed,
*   Corn-flowers peeping under?—*
Idle noons,
Lingering moons,
Sudden cloud,
Lightning's shroud,
Sudden rain,
Quick again
*   Smiles where late was thunder?—*
Are all these
Made to please?
*   So too is Pepíta.*

Autumn's prime,
Apple-time,
Smooth cheek round,
Heart all sound?—
Is it this
You would kiss?
*   Then it is Pepíta.*

You can bring
No sweet thing,

But my mind
Still shall find
 It is my Pepita.

Memory
Says to me
It is she—
She is fair
Past compare
 In the land of Tubal.

PEPITA (*seizing* JUAN'S *hand again*).
Oh, then, you do love me?

    JUAN.

      Yes, in the song.

    PEPITA (*sadly*).
Not out of it?—not love me out of it?

    JUAN.
Only a little out of it, my bird.
When I was singing I was Andrès, say,
Or one who loves you better still than he.

    PEPITA.

Not yourself?

    JUAN.
  No!

  PEPITA (*throwing his hand down pettishly*).
     Then take it back again!
I will not have it!

    JUAN.
    Listen, little one.
Juan is not a living man by himself:
His life is breathed in him by other men,

And they speak out of him.   He is their voice.
Juan's own life he gave once quite away.
Pepita's lover sang that song—not Juan.
We old, old poets, if we kept our hearts,
Should hardly know them from another man's.
They shrink to make room for the many more
We keep within us.   There, now—one more
      kiss,
And then go home again.

    PEPITA (*a little frightened, after letting* JUAN
        kiss her).

                You are not wicked ?

        JUAN.
Ask your confessor—tell him what I said.

(PEPITA *goes, while* JUAN *thrums his lute again,
   and sings.*)

       *Came a pretty maid
         By the moon's pure light,
     Loved me well, she said,
         Eyes with tears all bright,
          A pretty maid !*

       *But too late she strayed,
         Moonlight pure was there ;
     She was nought but shade
         Hiding the more fair,
          The heavenly maid !*

A vaulted room all stone. The light shed from a high lamp. Wooden chairs, a desk, book-shelves. The PRIOR, *in white frock, a black rosary with a crucifix of ebony and ivory at his side, is walking up and down, holding a written paper in his hands, which are clasped behind him.*

What if this witness lies? he says he heard her
Counting her blasphemies on a rosary,
And in a bold discourse with Salomo,
Say that the Host was nought but ill-mixed flour,
That it was mean to pray—she never prayed.
I know the man who wrote this for a cur,
Who follows Don Diego, sees life's good
In scraps my nephew flings to him.   What then?
Particular lies may speak a general truth.
I guess him false, but know her heretic—
Know her for Satan's instrument, bedecked
With heathenish charms, luring the souls of men
To damning trust in good unsanctified.
Let her be prisoned—questioned—she will give
Witness against herself, that were this false . . .

*(He looks at the paper again and reads, then
again thrusts it behind him.)*

The matter and the color are not false :
The form concerns the witness not the judge ;
For proof is gathered by the sifting mind,
Not given in crude and formal circumstance.
Suspicion is a heaven-sent lamp, and I—
I, watchman of the Holy Office, bear
That lamp in trust.   I will keep faithful watch.
The Holy Inquisition's discipline
Is mercy, saving her, if penitent—
God grant it !—else—root up the poison-plant,
Though 'twere a lily with a golden heart !

This spotless maiden with her pagan soul
Is the arch-enemy's trap : he turns his back
On all the prostitutes, and watches her
To see her poison men with false belief
In rebel virtues.   She has poisoned Silva :
His shifting mind, dangerous in fitfulness,
Strong in the contradiction of itself,
Carries his young ambitions wearily,
As holy vows regretted.   Once he seemed
The fresh-oped flower of Christian knighthood,
        born
For feats of holy daring ; and I said :
" That half of life which I, as monk, renounce,
Shall be fulfilled in him : Silva will be
That saintly noble, that wise warrior,
That blameless excellence in worldly gifts
I would have been, had I not asked to live
The higher life of man impersonal
Who reigns o'er all things by refusing all."
What is his promise now ?   Apostasy
From every high intent :—languid, nay, gone,
The prompt devoutness of a generous heart,
The strong obedience of a reverent will,
That breathes the Church's air and sees her light,
He peers and strains with feeble questioning,
Or else he jests.   He thinks I know it not—
I who have read the history of his lapse,
As clear as it is writ in the angel's book.
He will defy me—flings great words at me—
Me who have governed all our house's acts,
Since I, a stripling, ruled his stripling father.
This maiden is the cause, and if they wed,
The Holy War may count a captain lost.
For better he were dead than keep his place,
And fill it imfamously : in God's war
Slackness is infamy.   Shall I stand by
And let the tempter win ? defraud Christ's cause

And blot his banner ?—all for scruples weak
Of pity toward their young and frolicsome blood ;
Or nice discrimination of the tool
By which my hand shall work a sacred rescue ?
The fence of rules is for the purblind crowd ;
They walk by averaged precepts : sovereign men,
Seeing by God's light, see the general
By seeing all the special—own no rule
But their full vision of the moment's worth.
'Tis so God governs, using wicked men—
Nay, scheming fiends, to work his purposes.
Evil that good may come ?   Measure the good
Before you say what's evil.   Perjury ?
I scorn the perjurer, but I will use him
To serve the holy truth.   There is no lie
Save in his soul, and let his soul be judged.
I know the truth, and act upon the truth.

O God, thou knowest that my will is pure.
Thy servant owns nought for himself, his wealth
Is but obedience.   And I have sinned
In keeping small respects of human love—
Calling it mercy.   Mercy?   Where evil is
True mercy holds a sword.   Mercy would save.
Save whom ?   Save serpents, locusts, wolves ?
Or out of pity let the idiots gorge
Within a famished town ?   Or save the gains
Of men who trade in poison lest they starve ?
Save all things mean and foul that clog the earth
Stifling the better?   Save the fools who cling
For refuge round their hideous idol's limbs,
So leave the idol grinning unconsumed,
And save the fools to breed idolaters ?
O mercy worthy of the licking hound
That knows no future but its feeding-time !
Mercy has eyes that pierce the ages—sees
From heights divine of the eternal purpose

Far-scattered consequence in its vast sum ;
Chooses to save, but with illumined vision
Sees that to save is greatly to destroy.
'Tis so the Holy Inquisition sees : its wrath
Is fed from the strong heart of wisest love.
For love must needs make hatred.   He who loves
God and his law must hate the foes of God.
And I have sinned in being merciful :
Being slack in hate, I have been slack in love.

(*He takes the crucifix and holds it up before him.*)

Thou shuddering, bleeding, thirsting, dying God,
Thou Man of Sorrows, scourged and bruised and
          torn,
Suffering to save—wilt thou not judge the world ?
This arm which held the children, this pale hand
That gently touched the eyelids of the blind,
And opened passive to the cruel nail,
Shall one day stretch to leftward of thy throne,
Charged with the power that makes the lightning
          strong,
And hurl thy foes to everlasting hell.
And thou, Immaculate Mother, Virgin mild,
Thou sevenfold-pierced, thou pitying, pleading
          Queen,
Shalt see and smile, while the black filthy souls
Sink with foul weight to their eternal place,
Purging the Holy Light.   Yea, I have sinned
And called it mercy.   But I shrink no more.
To-morrow morn this temptress shall be safe
Under the Holy Inquisition's key.
He thinks to wed her, and defy me then,
She being shielded by our house's name.
But he shall never wed her.   I have said.

The time is come.   *Exurge, Domine,*
Judica causam tuam.   Let thy foes

Be driven as the smoke before the wind,
And melt like wax upon the furnace lip !

———

A large chamber richly furnished opening on a ter-
race-garden, the trees visible through the win-
dow in faint moonlight. Flowers hanging
about the window, lit up by the tapers. The
casket of jewels open on a table. The gold
necklace lying near. FEDALMA, *splendidly*
dressed and adorned with pearls aud rubies,
is walking up and down.

So soft a night was never made for sleep,
But for the waking of the finer sense
To every murmuring and gentle sound,
To subtlest odors, pulses, visitings
That touch our frames with wings too delicate
To be discerned amid the blare of day.

(*She pauses near the window to gather some*
jasmine : then walks again.)

Surely these flowers keep happy watch—their
    breath
Is the fond memory of the loving light.
I often rue the hours I lose in sleep :
It is a bliss too brief, only to see
This glorious world, to hear the voice of love,
To feel the touch, the breath of tenderness,
And then to rest as from a spectacle.
I need the curtained stillness of the night
To live through all my happy hours again
With more selection—cull them quite away
From blemished moments. Then in loneliness
The face that bent before me in the day
Rises in its own light, more vivid seems

Painted upon the dark, and ceaseless glows
With sweet solemnity of gazing love,
Till like the heavenly blue it seems to grow
Nearer, more kindred, and more cherishing,
Mingling with all my being.　　Then the words,
The tender low-toned words come back again,
With repetition welcome as the chime
Of softly hurrying brooks—" My only love—
My love while life shall last—my own Fedalma !"
Oh it is mine—the joy that once has been !
Poor eager hope is but a stammerer,
Must listen dumbly to great memory,
Who makes our bliss the sweeter by her telling.

　　　　　　(*She pauses a moment musingly.*)

But that dumb hope is still a sleeping guard
Whose quiet rhythmic breath saves me from
　　　dread
In this fair paradise.　　For if the earth
Broke off with flower-fringed edge, visibly sheer,
Leaving no footing for my forward step
But empty blackness . . .
　　　　　　　　　Nay, there is no fear—
They will renew themselves, day and my joy,
And all that past which is securely mine,
Will be the hidden root that nourishes
Our still unfolding, ever-ripening love !

　　(*While she is uttering the last words, a little bird
　　　falls softly on the floor behind her ; she hears
　　　the light sound of its fall, and turns round.*)

Did something enter ? . . .
　　　　　　　Yes, this little bird . . .
　　　　　　　　　(*She lifts it.*)

Dead and yet warm ; 'twas seeking sanctuary,
And died, perhaps of fright, at the altar foot.
Stay, there is something tied beneath the wing !

A strip of linen, streaked with blood — what
    blood?
The streaks are written words — are sent to me —
O God, art sent to me! *Dear child, Fedalma,*
Be brave, give no alarm — your Father comes !

              (*She lets the bird fall again.*)

My Father . . . comes . . . my Father . . .

  (*She turns in quivering expectation toward the*
    window. There is perfect stillness a few
    moments until ZARCA *appears at the win-*
    dow. He enters quickly and noiselessly;
    then stands still at his full height, and at
    a distance from FEDALMA.)

  FEDALMA (*in a low, distinct tone of terror*).

                It is he !
I said his fate had laid its hold on mine.

    ZARCA (*advancing a step or two*).
You know, then, who I am ?

      FEDALMA.
             The prisoner —
He whom I saw in fetters — and this neck-
    lace. . . .

      ZARCA.
Was played with by your fingers when it hung
About my neck, full fifteen years ago.

  FEDALMA (*looking at the necklace and handling*
    it, then speaking, as if unconsciously).
Full fifteen years ago !

      ZARCA.
           The very day
I lost you, when you wore a tiny gown
Of scarlet cloth with golden broidery :

'Twas clasped in front by coins—two golden
　　coins.
The one upon the left was split in two
Across the king's head, right from brow to nape,
A dent i' the middle nicking in the cheek.
You see I know the little gown by heart.

FEDALMA (*growing paler and more tremulous*).
Yes.　It is true—I have the gown—the clasps—
The braid—sore tarnished :—it is long ago !

ZARCA.
But yesterday to me ; for till to-day
I saw you always as that little child.
And when they took my necklace from me, still
Your fingers played about it on my neck,
And still those buds of fingers on your feet
Caught in its meshes as you seemed to climb
Up to my shoulder.　You were not stolen all.
You had a double life fed from my heart. . . .

　　(FEDALMA, *letting fall the necklace, makes
　　　an impulsive movement toward him, with
　　　outstretched hands.*)

The Gypsy father loves his children well.

FEDALMA (*shrinking, trembling, and letting fall
　　　　her hands*).

How came it that you sought me—no—I mean
How came it that you knew me—that you lost
　　me ?

ZARCA (*standing perfectly still*).
Poor child ! I see—your father and his rags
Are welcome as the piercing wintry wind
Within this silken chamber.　It is well.

I would not have a child who stooped to feign,
And aped a sudden love.   Better, true hate.

FEDALMA (*raising her eyes toward him, with a
flash of admiration, and looking at him fixedly*).

Father, how was it that we lost each other?

ZARCA.

I lost you as a man may lose a gem
Wherein he has compressed his total wealth,
Or the right hand whose cunning makes him
     great :
I lost you by a trivial accident.
Marauding Spaniards, sweeping like a storm
Over a spot within the Moorish bounds,
Near where our camp lay, doubtless snatched you
     up,
When Zind, your nurse, as she confessed, was
     urged
By burning thirst to wander toward the stream,
And leave you on the sand some paces off
Playing with pebbles, while she dog-like lapped.
'Twas so I lost you—never saw you more
Until to-day I saw you dancing !   Saw
The daughter of the Zincalo make sport
For those who spit upon her people's name.

FEDALMA (*vehemently*).

It was not sport.   What if the world looked
     on ?—
I danced for joy—for love of all the world.
But when you looked at me my joy was stabbed—
Stabbed with your pain.   I wondered . . . now
     I know . . .
It was my father's pain.

(*She pauses a moment with eyes bent down-
    ward, during which* ZARCA *examines
    her face.   Then she says quickly,*)
                How were you sure
At once I was your child?

ZARCA.

                        I had witness strong
As any Cadi needs, before I saw you!
I fitted all my memories with the chat
Of one named Juan—one whose rapid talk
Showers like the blossoms from a light-twigged
    shrub,
If you but cough beside it.   I learned all
The story of your Spanish nurture—all
The promise of your fortune.   When at last
I fronted you, my little maid full-grown,
Belief was turned to vision: then I saw
That she whom Spaniards called the bright Fe-
    dalma—
The little red-frocked foundling three years old—
Grown to such perfectness the Spanish Duke
Had wooed her for his Duchess—was the child,
Sole offspring of my flesh, that Lambra bore
One hour before the Christian, hunting us,
Hurried her on to death.   Therefore I sought—
Therefore I come to claim you—claim my child,
Not from the Spaniard, not from him who robbed,
But from herself.

(FEDALMA *has gradually approached close to*
    ZARCA, *and with a low sob sinks on her
    knees before him. He stoops to kiss her
    brow, and lays his hands on her head.*)
ZARCA (*with solemn tenderness*).

Tl.en my child owns her father?

FEDALMA.

Father! yes.
I will eat dust before I will deny
The flesh I spring from.

ZARCA.

There my daughter spoke.
Away then with these rubies!

(*He seizes the circlet of rubies and flings it on
the ground.* FEDALMA, *starting from
the ground with strong emotion, shrinks
backward.*)

Such a crown
Is infamy around a Zincala's brow.
It is her people's blood, decking her shame.

FEDALMA (*after a moment, slowly and distinctly,
as if accepting a doom.*)

Then . . . I was born . . . a Zincala?

ZARCA.

Of a blood
Unmixed as virgin wine-juice.

FEDALMA.

Of a race
More outcast and despised than Moor or Jew?

ZARCA.

Yes: wanderers whom no God took knowledge
of
To give them laws, to fight for them, or blight
Another race to make them ampler room;
Who have no Whence or Whither in their souls,

No dimmest lore of glorious ancestors
To make a common hearth for piety.

FEDALMA.

A race that lives on prey as foxes do
With stealthy, petty rapine : so despised,
It is not persecuted, only spurned,
Crushed underfoot, warred on by chance like rats,
Or swarming flies, or reptiles of the sea
Dragged in the net unsought, and flung far off
To perish as they may ?

ZARCA.

                          You paint us well.
So abject are the men whose blood we share :
Untutored, unbefriended, unendowed ;
No favorites of heaven or of men.
Therefore I cling to them !   Therefore no lure
Shall draw me to disown them, or forsake
The meagre wandering herd that lows for help
And needs me for its guide, to seek my pasture
Among the well-fed beeves that graze at will.
Because our race has no great memories,
I will so live, it shall remember me
For deeds of such divine beneficence
As rivers have, that teach men what is good
By blessing them.   I have been schooled—have
          caught
Lore from the Hebrew, deftness from the
          Moor—
Know the rich heritage, the milder life,
Of nations fathered by a mighty Past ;
But were our race accursed (as they who make
Good luck a god count all unlucky men)
I would espouse their curse sooner than take
My gifts from brethren naked of all good,
And lend them to the rich for usury.

(FEDALMA *again advances, and putting forth
her right hand grasps* ZARCA'S *left. He
places his other hand on her shoulder.
They stand so, looking at each other.*)

ZARCA.

And you, my child ? are you of other mind,
Choosing forgetfulness, hating the truth
That says you are akin to needy men ?—
Wishing your father were some Christian Duke,
Who would hang Gypsies when their task was
    done,
While you, his daughter, were not bound to
    care ?

FEDALMA (*in a troubled, eager voice*).

No, I should always care—I cared for you—
For all, before I dreamed . . . .

ZARCA.

                Before you dreamed
That you were born a Zíncala—your flesh
Stamped with your people's faith.

FEDALMA (*bitterly*).

                The Gypsies' faith ?
Men say they have none.

ZARCA.

                Oh, it is a faith
Taught by no priest, but by their beating hearts :
Faith to each other : the fidelity
Of fellow-wanderers in a desert place
Who share the same dire thirst, and therefore
    share
The scanty water : the fidelity
Of men whose pulses leap with kindred fire,

Who in the flash of eyes, the clasp of hands,
The speech that even in lying tells the truth
Of heritage inevitable as birth,
Nay, in the silent bodily presence feel
The mystic stirring of a common life
Which makes the many one : fidelity
To the consecrating oath our sponsor Fate
Made through our infant breath when we were
      born
The fellow-heirs of that small island, Life,
Where we must dig and sow and reap with
      brothers.
Fear thou that oath, my daughter—nay, not
      fear,
But love it ; for the sanctity of oaths
Lies not in lightning that avenges them,
But in the injury wrought by broken bonds
And in the garnered good of human trust.
And you have sworn—even with your infant
      breath
You too were pledged . . . .

FEDALMA (*letting go* ZARCA'S *hand, and sinking
    backward on her knees, with bent head, as if
    before some impending crushing weight*).

             To what ? what have I sworn ?

               ZARCA.

To take the heirship of the Gypsy's child :
The child of him who, being chief, will be
The savior of his tribe, or if he fail
Will choose to fail rather than basely win
The prize of renegades.   Nay, will not choose—
Is there a choice for strong souls to be weak ?
For men erect to crawl like hissing snakes ?
I choose not—I *am* Zarca.   Let him choose
Who halts and wavers, having appetite

To feed on garbage.   You, my child—are you
Halting and wavering ?

FEDALMA (*raising her head*).

Say what is my task.

ZARCA.

To be the angel of a homeless tribe :
To help me bless a race taught by no prophet,
And make their name, now but a badge of scorn,
A glorious banner floating in their midst,
Stirring the air they breathe with impulses
Of generous pride, exalting fellowship
Until it soars to magnanimity.
I'll guide my brethren forth to their new land,
Where they shall plant and sow and reap their
        own,
Serving each other's needs, and so be spurred
To skill in all the arts that succor life ;
Where we may kindle our first altar-fire
From settled hearths, and call our Holy Place
The hearth that binds us in one family.
That land awaits them : they await their chief—
Me who am prisoned.   All depends on you.

FEDALMA (*rising to her full height, and looking
        solemnly at* ZARCA).

Father, your child is ready ! She will not
Forsake her kindred : she will brave all scorn
Sooner than scorn herself.   Let Spaniards all,
Christians, Jews, Moors, shoot out the lip and
        say,
" Lo, the first hero in a tribe of thieves."
Is it not written so of them ? They, too,
Were slaves, lost, wandering, sunk beneath a
        curse,
Till Moses, Christ, and Mahomet were born,
Till beings lonely in their greatness lived,

And lived to save their people.   Father, listen.
The Duke to-morrow weds me secretly :
But straight he will present me as his wife
To all his household, cavaliers and dames
And noble pages.   Then I will declare
Before them all, " I am his daughter, his,
The Gypsy's, owner of this golden badge.'
Then I shall win your freedom ; then the Duke—
Why, he will be your son !—will send you forth
With aid and honors.   Then, before all eyes
I'll clasp this badge on you, and lift my brow
For you to kiss it, saying by that sign,
" I glory in my father."   This, to-morrow.

                    ZARCA.

A woman's dream—who thinks by smiling well
To ripen figs in frost.   What ! marry first,
And then proclaim your birth ? Enslave your-
            self
To use your freedom ?   Share another's name,
Then treat it as you will ?   How will that tune
Ring in your bridegroom's ears—that sudden
            song
Of triumph in your Gypsy father ?

              FEDALMA (*discouraged*).
                                    Nay,
I meant not so.   We marry hastily—
Yet there is time—there will be :—in less space
Than he can take to look at me, I'll speak
And tell him all.   Oh, I am not afraid !
His love for me is stronger than all hate ;
Nay, stronger than my love, which cannot sway
Demons that haunt me—tempt me to rebel.
Were he Fedalma and I Silva, he
Could love confession, prayers, and tonsured
            monks

If my soul craved them.   He will never hate
The race that bore him what he loves the most.
I shall but do more strongly what I will,
Having his will to help me.   And to-morrow,
Father, as surely as this heart shall beat,
You—every Gypsy chained, shall be set free.

ZARCA (*coming   nearer   to   her,   and   laying   his
               hand on her shoulder*).

Too late, too poor a service that, my child !
Not so the woman who would save her tribe
Must help its heroes—not by wordy breath,
By easy prayers strong in a lover's ear,
By showering wreaths and sweets and wafted
          kisses,
And then, when all the smiling work is done,
Turning to rest upon her down again,
And whisper languid pity for her race
Upon the bosom of her alien spouse.
Not to such petty mercies as can fall
'Twixt stitch and stitch of silken broidery,
Such miracles of mitred saints who pause
Beneath their gilded canopy to heal
A man sun-stricken : not to such trim merit
As soils its dainty shoes for charity
And simpers meekly at the pious stain,
But never trod with naked bleeding feet
Where no man praised it, and where no Church
          blessed :
Not to such almsdeeds fit for holidays
Were you, my daughter, consecrated—bound
By laws that, breaking, you will dip your bread
In murdered brother's blood and call it sweet—
When you were born beneath the dark man's
          tent,
And lifted up in sight of all your tribe,
Who greeted you with shouts of loyal joy,

Sole offspring of the chief in whom they trust
As in the oft-tried never-failing flint
They strike their fire from.   Other work is yours.

FEDALMA.

What work ?—what is it that you ask of me ?

ZARCA.

A work as pregnant as the act of men
Who set their ships aflame and spring to land,
A fatal deed . . . .

FEDALMA.

        Stay ! never utter it !
If it can part my lot from his whose love
Has chosen me.   Talk not of oaths, of birth,
Of men as numerous as the dim white stars—
As cold and distant, too, for my heart's pulse.
No ills on earth, though you should count them
    up
With grains to make a mountain, can outweigh
For me, his ill who is my supreme love.
All sorrows else are but imagined flames, .
Making me shudder at an unfelt smart ;
But his imagined sorrow is a fire
That scorches me.

ZARCA.

       I know, I know it well—
The first young passionate wail of spirits called
To some great destiny.   In vain, my daughter !
Lay the young eagle in what nest you will,
The cry and swoop of eagles overhead
Vibrate prophetic in its kindred frame,
And make it spread its wings and poise itself
For the eagle's flight.   Hear what you have
    to do.

(FEDALMA *stands half averted, as if she
dreaded the effect of his looks and words.*)

My comrades even now file off their chains
In a low turret by the battlements,
Where we were locked with slight and sleepy
        guard—
We who had files hid in our shaggy hair,
And possible ropes that waited but our will
In half our garments.   Oh, the Moorish blood
Runs thick and warm to us, though thinned by
        chrism.
I found a friend among our jailers—one
Who loves the Gypsy as the Moor's ally.
I know the secrets of this fortress.   Listen.
Hard by yon terrace is a narrow stair,
Cut in the living rock, and at one point
In its slow straggling course it branches off
Toward a low wooden door, that art has bossed
To such unevenness, it seems one piece
With the rough-hewn rock.   Open that door, it
        leads
Through a broad passage burrowed under-
        ground.
A good half-mile out to the open plain :
Made for escape, in dire extremity
From siege or burning, of the house's wealth
In women or in gold.   To find that door
Needs one who knows the number of the steps
Just to the turning-point ; to open it,
Needs one who knows the secret of the bolt.
You have that secret : you will ope that door,
And fly with us.

FEDALMA (*receding a little, and gathering herself
    up in an attitude of resolve opposite to* ZARCA).

            No, I will never fly !
Never forsake that chief half of my soul

Where lies my love.   I swear to set you free.
Ask for no more ; it is not possible.
Father, my soul is not too base to ring
At touch of your great thoughts ; nay, in my
    blood
There streams the sense unspeakable of kind,
As leopard feels at ease with leopard.   But—
Look at these hands !   You say when they were
    little
They played about the gold upon your neck.
I do believe it, for their tiny pulse
Made record of it in the inmost coil
Of growing memory.   But see them now !
Oh, they have made fresh record; twined them-
    selves
With other throbbing hands whose pulses feed
Not memories only but a blended life—
Life that will bleed to death if it be severed.
Have pity on me, father !   Wait the morning ;
Say you will wait the morning.   I will win
Your freedom openly : you shall go forth
With aid and honors.   Silva will deny
Nought to my asking . . . .

    ZARCA (*with contemptuous decision*).

                 Till you ask him aught
Wherein he is powerless.   Soldiers even now
Murmur against him that he risks the town,
And forfeits all the prizes of a foray
To get his bridal pleasure with a bride
Too low for him.   They'll murmur more and
    louder
If captives of our pith and sinew, fit
For all the work the Spaniard hates, are freed—
Now, too, when Spanish hands are scanty.
    What,
Turn Gypsies loose instead of hanging them !

'Tis flat against the edict.   Nay, perchance
Murmurs aloud may turn to silent threats
Of some well-sharpened dagger ; for your Duke
Has to his heir a pious cousin, who deems
The Cross were better served if he were Duke.
Such   good   you'll   work   your   lover   by   your
        prayers.

FEDALMA.

Then, I will free you now !   You shall be safe,
Nor he be blamed, save for his love to me.
I will declare what I have done : the deed
May put our marriage off . . . .

ZARCA.

                        Ay, till the time
When you shall be a queen in Africa,
And he be prince enough to sue for you.
You cannot free us and come back to him.

FEDALMA.

And why ?

ZARCA.

        I would compel you to go forth.

FEDALMA.

You tell me that ?

ZARCA.

                Yes, for I'd have you choose ;
Though, being of the blood you are—my blood—
You have no right to choose.

FEDALMA.

                        I only owe
A daughter's debt ; I was not born a slave.

ZARCA.

No, not a slave ; but you were born to reign.
'Tis a compulsion of a higher sort,
Whose fetters are the net invisible
That hold all life together.   Royal deeds
May make long destinies for multitudes,
And you are called to do them.   You belong
Not to the petty round of circumstance
That makes a woman's lot, but to your tribe,
Who trust in me and in my blood with trust
That men call blind ; but it is only blind
As unyeaned reason is, that grows and stirs
Within the womb of superstition.

FEDALMA.

              No !
I belong to him who loves me—whom I love—
Who chose me—whom I chose—to whom I
      pledged
A woman's truth.   And that is nature too,
Issuing a fresher law than laws of birth.

ZARCA.

Unmake yourself, then, from a Zincala—
Unmake yourself from being child of mine !
Take holy water, cross your dark skin white ;
Round your proud eyes to foolish kitten looks ;
Walk mincingly, and smirk, and twitch your
      robe :
Unmake yourself—doff all the eagle plumes
And be a parrot, chained to a ring that slips
Upon a Spaniard's thumb, at will of his
That you should prattle o'er his words again !
Get a small heart that flutters at the smiles
Of that plump penitent, that greedy saint
Who breaks all treaties in the name of God,

Saves souls by confiscation, sends to heaven
The altar-fumes of burning heretics,
And chaffers with the Levite for the gold ;
Holds Gypsies beasts unfit for sacrifice,
So sweeps them out like worms alive or dead.
Go, trail your gold and velvet in her court !—
A conscious Zíncala, smile at your rare luck,
While half your brethren . . . .

FEDALMA.

                I am not so vile !
It is not to such mockeries that I cling,
Not to the flaring tow of gala-lights ;
It is to him—my love—the face of day.

ZARCA.

What, will you part him from the air he breathes,
Never inhale with him although you kiss him ?
Will you adopt a soul without its thoughts,
Or grasp a life apart from flesh and blood ?
Till then you cannot wed a Spanish Duke
And not wed shame at mention of your race,
And not wed hardness to their miseries—
Nay, not wed murder.   Would you save my life
Yet stab my purpose ? maim my every limb,
Put out my eyes, and turn me loose to feed ?
Is that salvation ? rather drink my blood.
That child of mine who weds my enemy—
Adores a God who took no heed of Gypsies—
Forsakes her people, leaves their poverty
To join the luckier crowd that mocks their woes—
That child of mine is doubly murderess,
Murdering her father's hope, her people's trust.
Such draughts are mingled in your cup of love !
And when you have become a thing so poor,
Your life is all a fashion without law
Save frail conjecture of a changing wish,

Your worshipped sun, your smiling face of day,
Will turn to cloudiness, and you will shiver
In your thin finery of vain desire.
Men call his passion madness; and he, too,
May learn to think it madness: 'tis a thought
Of ducal sanity.

FEDALMA.

                    No, he is true!
And if I part from him I part from joy.
Oh, it was morning with us—I seemed young.
But now I know I am an aged sorrow—
My people's sorrow.   Father, since I am yours—
Since I must walk an unslain sacrifice,
Carrying the knife within me, quivering—
Put cords upon me, drag me to the doom
My birth has laid upon me.   See, I kneel:
I cannot will to go.

ZARCA.

                    Will then to stay!
Say you will take your better, painted such
By blind desire, and choose the hideous worse
For thousands who were happier but for you.
My thirty followers are assembled now
Without this terrace: I your father wait
That you may lead us forth to liberty—
Restore me to my tribe—five hundred men
Whom I alone can save, alone can rule,
And plant them as a mighty nation's seed.
Why, vagabonds who clustered round one man,
Their voice of God, their prophet and their king,
Twice grew to empire on the teeming shores
Of Africa, and sent new royalties
To feed afresh the Arab sway in Spain.
My vagabonds are a seed more generous,
Quick as the serpent, loving as the hound,

And beautiful as disinherited gods.
They have a promised land beyond the sea :
There I may lead them, raise my standard, call
The wandering Zíncali to that new home,
And make a nation—bring light, order, law,
Instead of chaos.   You, my only heir,
Are called to reign for me when I am gone.
Now choose your deed : to save or to destroy.
You, a born Zíncala, you, fortunate
Above your fellows—you who hold a curse
Or blessing in the hollow of your hand—
Say you will loose that hand from fellowship,
Let go the rescuing rope, hurl all the tribes,
Children and countless beings yet to come,
Down from the upward path of light and joy,
Back to the dark and marshy wilderness
Where life is nought but blind tenacity
Of that which is.   Say you will curse your race !

FEDALMA (*rising and stretching out her arms in
                          deprecation*).

No, no—I will not say it—I will go !
Father, I choose !   I will not take a heaven
Haunted by shrieks of far-off misery.
This deed and I have ripened with the hours :
It is a part of me—a wakened thought
That, rising like a giant, masters me,
And grows into a doom.   O mother life,
That seemed to nourish me so tenderly,
Even in the womb you vowed me to the fire,
Hung on my soul the burden of men's hopes,
And pledged me to redeem !—I'll pay the debt.
You gave me strength that I should pour it all
Into this anguish.   I can never shrink
Back into bliss—my heart has grown too big
With things that might be.   Father, I will go.
I will strip off these gems.   Some happier bride

Shall wear them, since Fedalma would be dowered
With nought but curses, dowered with misery
Of men—of women, who have hearts to bleed
As hers is bleeding.

> *(She sinks on a seat, and begins to take off
> her jewels.)*
> Now, good gems, we part.

Speak of me always tenderly to Silva.

> *(She pauses, turning to* ZARCA.*)*

O father, will the women of our tribe
Suffer as I do, in the years to come
When you have made them great in Africa?
Redeemed from ignorant ills only to feel
A conscious woe?   Then—is it worth the pains?
Were it not better when we reach that shore
To raise a funeral-pile and perish all,
So closing up a myriad avenues
To misery yet unwrought?   My soul is faint—
Will these sharp pangs buy any certain good?

ZARCA.

Nay, never falter : no great deed is done
By falterers who ask for certainty.
No good is certain, but the steadfast mind,
The undivided will to seek the good :
'Tis that compels the elements, and wrings
A human music from the indifferent air.
The greatest gift the hero leaves his race
Is to have been a hero.   Say we fail !—
We feed the high tradition of the world
And leave our spirit in our children's breasts.

FEDALMA (*unclasping her jewelled belt, and throwing it down*).

Yes, say that we shall fail !   I will not count
On aught but being faithful.   I will take

This yearning self of mine and strangle it.
I will not be half-hearted : never yet
Fedalma did aught with a wavering soul.
Die, my young joy—die, all my hungry hopes—
The milk you cry for from the breast of life
Is thick with curses.   Oh, all fatness here
Snatches   its   meat   from   leanness—feeds   on
      graves.
I will seek nothing but to shun base joy.
The saints were cowards who stood by to see
Christ crucified : they should have flung them-
      selves
Upon the Roman spears, and died in vain—
The grandest death, to die in vain—for love
Greater than sways the forces of the world !
That death shall be my bridegroom.   I will wed
The curse that blights my people.   Father, come !

ZARCA.

No curse has fallen on us till we cease
To help each other.   You, if you are false
To that first fellowship, lay on the curse.
But write now to the Spaniard : briefly say
That I, your father, came ; that you obeyed
The fate which made you Zíncala, as his fate
Made him a Spanish duke and Christian knight.
He must not think . . .

FEDALMA.

                    Yes, I will write, but he—
Oh, he would know it—he would never think
The chain that dragged me from him could be
      aught
But scorching iron entering in my soul.

                              (*She writes.*)

Silva, sole love—he came—my father came.
I am the daughter of the Gypsy chief

Who means to be the Saviour of our tribe.
He calls on me to live for his great end.
To live? nay, die for it. Fedalma dies
In leaving Silva : all that lives henceforth
Is the poor Zíncala.   (*She rises.*)

             Father, now I go
To wed my people's lot.

ZARCA.

                To wed a crown.
Our people's lowly lot we will make royal—
Give it a country, homes, and monuments
Held sacred through the lofty memories
That we shall leave behind us. Come, my
     Queen !

FEDALMA.

Stay, my betrothal ring !—one kiss—farewell !
O love, you were my crown. No other crown
Is aught but thorns on my poor woman's brow.

BOOK II.

SILVA was marching homeward while the moon
Still shed mild brightness like the far-off hope
Of those pale virgin lives that wait and pray.
The stars thin-scattered made the heavens large,
Bending in slow procession ; in the east
Emergent from the dark waves of the hills,
Seeming a little sister of the moon,
Glowed Venus all unquenched.   Silva, in haste,
Exultant and yet anxious, urged his troop
To quick and quicker march : he had delight
In forward stretching shadows, in the gleams
That travelled on the armor of the van,
And in the many-hoofed sound : in all that told
Of hurrying movement to o'ertake his thought
Already in Bedmár, close to Fedalma,
Leading her forth a wedded bride, fast vowed,
Defying Father Isidor.   His glance
Took in with much content the priest who rode
Firm in his saddle, stalwart and broad-backed,
Crisp-curled, and comfortably secular,
Right in the front of him.   But by degrees
Stealthily faint, disturbing with slow loss
That showed not yet full promise of a gain,
The light was changing, and the watch intense
Of moon and stars seemed weary, shivering :
The sharp white brightness passed from off the
        rocks
Carrying the shadows : beauteous Night lay dead
Under the pall of twilight, and the love-star

Sickened and shrank. The troop was winding
    now
Upward to where a pass between the peaks
Seemed like an opened gate—to Silva seemed
An outer-gate of heaven, for through that pass
They entered his own valley, near Bedmár.
Sudden within the pass a horseman rose,
One instant dark upon the banner pale
Of rock-cut sky, the next in motion swift
With hat and plume high shaken—ominous.
Silva had dreamed his future, and the dream
Held not this messenger.   A minute more—
It was his friend Don Alvar whom he saw
Reining his horse up, face to face with him,
Sad as the twilight, all his clothes ill-girt—
As if he had been roused to see one die,
And brought the news to him whom death had
    robbed.
Silva believed he saw the worse—the town
Stormed by the infidel—or, could it be
Fedalma dragged ?—no, there was not yet time.
But with a marble face, he only said,
" What evil, Alvar ?"

                " What this paper speaks."
It was Fedalma's letter folded close
And mute as yet for Silva.   But his friend
Keeping it still sharp-pinched against his breast,
" It will smite hard, my lord : a private grief.
I would not have you pause to read it here.
Let us ride on—we use the moments best,
Reaching the town with speed.   The smaller ill
Is that our Gypsy prisoners have escaped."
" No more.   Give me the paper—nay, I know—
'Twill make no difference.   Bid them march on
    faster."
Silva pushed forward—held the paper crushed
Close in his right.   " They have imprisoned her,"

He said to Alvar in low, hard-cut tones,
Like a dream-speech of slumbering revenge.
" No—when they came to fetch her she was gone."
Swift as the right touch on a spring, that word
Made Silva read the letter.   She was gone !
But not into locked darkness—only gone
Into free air—where he might find her yet.
The bitter loss had triumph in it—what !
They would have seized her with their holy claws,
The Prior's sweet morsel of despotic hate
Was snatched from off his lips.   This misery
Had yet a taste of joy.
                              But she was gone !
The sun had risen, and in the castle walls
The light grew strong and stronger.   Silva
          walked
Through the long corridor where dimness yet
Cherished a lingering, flickering, dying hope :
Fedalma still was there—he could not see
The vacant place that once her presence filled.
Can we believe that the dear dead are gone ?
Love in sad weeds forgets the funeral day,
Opens the chamber door and almost smiles—
Then sees the sunbeams pierce athwart the bed
Where the pale face is not.   So Silva's joy,
Like the sweet habit of caressing hands
That seek the memory of another hand,
Still lived on fitfully in spite of words,
And, numbing thought with vague illusion, dulled
The slow and steadfast beat of certainty.
But in the rooms inexorable light
Streamed through the opened window where she
          fled,
Streamed on the belt and coronet thrown down—
Mute witnesses—sought out the typic ring
That sparkled on the crimson, solitary,
Wounding him like a word.   O hateful light !

It filled the chambers with her absence, glared
On all the motionless things her hand had
        touched,
Motionless all—save where old Iñez lay
Sunk on the floor holding her rosary,
Making its shadow tremble with her fear.
And Silva passed her by because she grieved :
It was the lute, the gems, the pictured heads,
He longed to crush, because they made no sign
But of insistence that she was not there,
She who had filled his sight and hidden them.
He went forth on the terrace tow'rd the stairs,
Saw the rained petals of the cistus flowers
Crushed by large feet ; but on one shady spot
Far down the steps, where dampness made a
        home,
He saw a footprint delicate-slippered, small,
So dear to him, he searched for sister-prints,
Searched in the rock-hewn passage with a lamp
For other trace of her, and found a glove ;
But not Fedalma's.   It was Juan's glove,
Tasselled, perfumed, embroidered with his name,
A gift of dames.   Then Juan, too, was gone ?
Full-mouthed conjecture, hurrying through the
        town,
Had spread the tale already : it was he
That helped the Gypsies' flight.   He talked and
        sang
Of nothing but the Gypsies and Fedalma.
He drew the threads together, wove the plan ;
Had lingered out by moonlight, had been seen
Strolling, as was his wont, within the walls,
Humming his ditties.   So Don Alvar told,
Conveying outside rumor.   But the Duke,
Making of haughtiness a visor closed,
Would show no agitated front in quest
Of small disclosures.   What her writing bore

Had been enough.   He knew that she was gone,
Knew why.
      " The Duke," some said, "will send a force,
Retake the prisoners, and bring back his bride."
But others, winking, " Nay, her wedding dress
Would be the *san-benito*.   'Tis a fight
Between the Duke and Prior.   Wise bets will
            choose
The   churchman :   he's   the   iron,   and   the
            Duke . . ."
" Is a fine piece of pottery," said mine host,
Softening the sarcasm with a bland regret.

There was the thread that in the new-made knot
Of obstinate circumstance seemed hardest drawn,
Vexed most the sense of Silva, in these hours
Of fresh and angry pain—there, in that fight
Against a foe whose sword was magical,
His shield invisible terrors—against a foe
Who stood as if upon the smoking mount
Ordaining plagues.   All else, Fedalma's flight,
The father's claim, her Gypsy birth disclosed,
Were momentary crosses, hindrances
A Spanish noble might despise.   This Chief
Might still be treated with, would not refuse
A proffered ransom, which would better serve
Gypsy prosperity, give him more power
Over his tribe, than any fatherhood :
Nay, all the father in him must plead loud
For marriage of his daughter where she loved—
Her love being placed so high and lustrously.
The Gypsy chieftain had foreseen a price
That   would   be   paid   him   for   his   daughter's
            dower—
Might soon give signs.   Oh, all his purpose lay
Face upward.   Silva here felt strong, and smiled.
What could a Spanish noble not command ?

He only helped the Queen, because he chose ;
Could war on Spaniards, and could spare the
        Moor ;
Buy justice, or defeat it—if he would :
Was loyal, not from weakness but from strength
Of high resolve to use his birthright well.
For nobles too are gods, like emperors,
Accept perforce their own divinity,
And wonder at the virtue of their touch,
Till obstinate resistance shakes their creed,
Shattering that self whose wholeness is not
        rounded
Save in the plastic souls of other men.
Don Silva had been suckled in that creed
(A high-taught speculative noble else),
Held it absurd as foolish argument
If any failed in deference, was too proud
Not to be courteous to so poor a knave
As one who knew not necessary truths
Of birth and dues of rank ; but cross his will,
The miracle-working will, his rage leaped out
As by a right divine to rage more fatal
Than a mere mortal man's.   And now that will
Had met a stronger adversary—strong
As awful ghosts are whom we cannot touch,
While they clutch *us*, subtly as poisoned air,
In deep-laid fibres of inherited fear
That lie below all courage.
                              Silva said,
" She is not lost to me, might still be mine
But for the Inquisition—the dire hand
That waits to clutch her with a hideous grasp
Not passionate, human, living, but a grasp
As in the death-throe when the human soul
Departs and leaves force unrelenting, locked,
Not to be loosened save by slow decay
That frets the universe.   Father Isidor

Has willed it so : his phial dropped the oil
To catch the air-borne motes of idle slander ;
He fed the fascinated gaze that clung
Round all her movements, frank as growths of
    spring,
With the new hateful interest of suspicion.
What barrier is this Gypsy ? a mere gate
I'll find the key for.   The one barrier,
The tightening cord that winds about my limbs,
Is this kind uncle, this imperious saint,
He who will save me, guard me from myself.
And he can work his will : I have no help
Save reptile secrecy, and no revenge
Save that I *will* do what he schemes to hinder.
Ay, secrecy, and disobedience—these
No tyranny can master.   Disobey !
You may divide the universe with God,
Keeping your will unbent, and hold a world
Where He is not supreme.   The Prior shall know
    it !
His will shall breed resistance : he shall do
The thing he would not, further what he hates
By hardening my resolve."

                     But 'neath this speech—
Defiant, hectoring, the more passionate voice
Of many-blended consciousness—there breathed
Murmurs of doubt, the weakness of a self
That is not one ; denies and yet believes ;
Protests with passion, " This is natural "—
Yet owns the other still were truer, better,
Could nature follow it : a self disturbed
By budding growths of reason premature
That breed disease.   With all his outflung rage
Silva half shrank before the steadfast man
Whose life was one compacted whole, a realm
Where the rule changed not, and the law was
    strong.

Then that reluctant homage stirred new hate,
And gave rebellion an intenser will.

But soon this inward strife the slow-paced hours
Slackened ; and the soul sank with hunger-pangs,
Hunger of love.　Debate was swept right down
By certainty of loss intolerable.
A little loss ! only a dark-tressed maid
Who had no heritage save her beauteous being !
But in the candor of her virgin eyes
Saying, I love ; and in the mystic charm
Of her dear presence, Silva found a heaven
Where faith and hope were drowned as stars in
　　　day.
Fedalma there, each momentary Now
Seemed a whole blest existence, a full cup
That, flowing over, asked no pouring hand
From past to future.　All the world was hers.
Splendor was but the herald trumpet-note
Of her imperial coming : penury
Vanished before her as before a gem,
The pledge of treasuries.　Fedalma there,
He thought all loveliness was lovelier,
She crowning it : all goodness credible,
Because of that great trust her goodness bred.
For the strong current of the passionate love
Which urged his life tow'rd hers, like urgent floods
That hurry through the various-mingled earth,
Carried within its stream all qualities
Of what it penetrated, and made love
Only another name, as Silva was,
For the whole man that breathed within his frame.
And she was gone.　Well, goddesses will go ;
But for a noble there were mortals left
Shaped just like goddesses—O hateful sweet !
O impudent pleasure that should dare to front
With vulgar visage memories divine !

The noble's birthright of miraculous will
Turning *I would* to *must be*, spurning all
Offered as substitute for what it chose,
Tightened and fixed in strain irrevocable
The passionate selection of that love
Which came not first but as all-conquering last.
Great Love has many attributes, and shrines
For varied worship, but his force divine
Shows most its many-named fulness in the man
Whose nature multitudinously mixed—
Each ardent impulse grappling with a thought—
Resists all easy gladness, all content
Save mystic rapture, where the questioning soul
Flooded with consciousness of good that is
Finds life one bounteous answer.   So it was
In Silva's nature, Love had mastery there,
Not as a holiday ruler, but as one
Who quells a tumult in a day of dread,
A welcomed despot.

          O all comforters,
All soothing things that bring mild ecstasy,
Came with her coming, in her presence lived.
Spring afternoons, when delicate shadows fall
Pencilled upon the grass ; high summer morns
When white light rains upon the quiet sea
And corn-fields flush with ripeness ; odors soft—
Dumb vagrant bliss that seems to seek a home
And find it deep within, 'mid stirrings vague
Of far-off moments when our life was fresh ;
All sweetly-tempered music, gentle change
Of sound, form, color, as on wild lagoons
At sunset when from black far-floating prows
Comes a clear wafted song ; all exquisite joy
Of a subdued desire, like some strong stream
Made placid in the fulness of a lake—
All came with her sweet presence, for she brought
The love supreme which gathers to its realm

All powers of loving.   Subtle nature's hand
Waked with a touch the far-linked harmonies
In her own manifold work.   Fedalma there,
Fastidiousness became the prelude fine
For full contentment ; and young melancholy,
Lost for its origin, seemed but the pain
Of waiting for that perfect happiness.
The happiness was gone !
                                    He sate alone,
Hating companionship that was not hers ;
Felt bruised with hopeless longing ; drank, as
        wine,
Illusions of what had been, would have been ;
Weary with anger and a strained resolve,
Sought passive happiness in waking dreams.
It has been so with rulers, emperors,
Nay, sages who held secrets of great Time,
Sharing his hoary and beneficent life—
Men who sate throned among the multitudes—
They have sore sickened at the loss of one.
Silva sat lonely in her chamber, leaned
Where she had leaned, to feel the evening breath
Shed from the orange trees ; when suddenly
His grief was echoed in a sad young voice
Far and yet near, brought by aërial wings.

The world is great : the birds all fly from me,
The stars are golden fruit upon a tree
All out of reach : my little sister went,
                And I am lonely.

The world is great : I tried to mount the hill
Above the pines, where the light lies so still,
But it rose higher : little Lisa went,
                And I am lonely.

The world is great : the wind comes rushing by,
I wonder where it comes from ; sea-birds cry

And hurt my heart : my little sister went,
And I am lonely.

The world is great : the people laugh and talk,
And make loud holiday : how fast they walk !
I'm lame, they push me : little Lisa went,
And I am lonely.

'Twas Pablo, like the wounded spirit of song
Pouring melodious pain to cheat the hour
For idle soldiers in the castle court.
Dreamily Silva heard and hardly felt
The song was outward, rather felt it part
Of his own aching, like the lingering day,
Or slow and mournful cadence of the bell.
But when the voice had ceased he longed for it,
And fretted at the pause, as memory frets
When words that made its body fall away
And leave it yearning dumbly.   Silva then
Bethought him whence the voice came, framed
          perforce
Some outward image of a life not his
That made a sorrowful centre to the world :
A boy lame, melancholy-eyed, who bore
A viol—yes, that very child he saw
This morning eating roots by the gateway—saw
As one fresh-ruined sees and spells a name
And knows not what he does, yet finds it writ
Full in the inner record.   Hark, again !
The voice and viol.   Silva called his thought
To guide his ear and track the travelling sound.

O bird that used to press
Thy head against my cheek
With touch that seemed to speak
And ask a tender " yes "—
Ay de mi, my bird !

O tender downy breast
And warmly beating heart,
That beating seemed a part
Of me who gave it rest—
Ay de mi, my bird!

The western court !   The singer might be seen
From the upper gallery : quick the Duke was
        there
Looking upon the court as on a stage.
Men eased of armor, stretched upon the ground,
Gambling by snatches ; shepherds from the hills
Who brought their bleating friends for slaughter ;
        grooms
Shouldering   loose   harness ;   leather-aproned
        smiths,
Traders with wares, green-suited serving-men,
Made a round audience ; and in their midst
Stood little Pablo, pouring forth his song,
Just as the Duke had pictured.   But the song
Was strangely companied by Roldan's play
With the swift gleaming balls, and now was
        crushed
By peals of laughter at grave Annibal,
Who carrying stick and purse o'erturned the
        pence
Making mistake by rule.   Silva had thought
To melt hard bitter grief by fellowship
With the world-sorrow trembling in his ear
In Pablo's voice ; had meant to give command
For the boy's presence ; but this company,
This mountebank and monkey, must be—stay !
Not be excepted—must be ordered too
Into his private presence ; they had brought
Suggestion of a ready shapen tool
To cut a path between his helpless wish
And what it imaged.   A ready shapen tool !

A spy, an envoy whom he might despatch
In unsuspected secrecy, to find
The Gypsies' refuge so that none beside
Might learn it.   And this juggler could be
     bribed,
Would have no fear of Moors—for who would
     kill
Dancers and monkeys ?—could pretend a journey
Back to his home, leaving his boy the while
To please the Duke with song.   Without such
     chance—
An envoy cheap and secret as a mole
Who could go scatheless, come back for his pay
And vanish straight, tied by no neighborhood—
Without such chance as this poor juggler brought,
Finding Fedalma was betraying her.

Short interval betwixt the thought and deed.
Roldan was called to private audience
With Annibal and Pablo.   All the world
(By which I mean the score or two who heard)
Shrugged high their shoulders, and supposed the
     Duke
Would fain beguile the evening and replace
His lacking happiness, as was the right
Of nobles, who could pay for any cure,
And wore nought broken, save a broken limb.
In truth, at first, the Duke bade Pablo sing,
But, while he sang, called Roldan wide apart,
And told him of a mission secret, brief—
A quest which well performed might earn much
     gold,
But, if betrayed, another sort of pay.
Roldan was ready ; '' wished above all for gold
And never wished to speak ; had worked enough
At wagging his old tongue and chiming jokes ;
Thought it was others' turn to play the fool.

Give him but pence enough, no rabbit, sirs,
Would eat and stare and be more dumb than
       he.
Give him his orders."
                    They were given straight ;
Gold for the journey, and to buy a mule
Outside the gates through which he was to pass
Afoot and carelessly.   The boy would stay
Within the castle, at the Duke's command,
And must have nought but ignorance to betray
For threats or coaxing.   Once the quest per-
       formed,
The news delivered with some pledge of truth
Safe to the Duke, the juggler should go forth,
A fortune in his girdle, take his boy
And settle firm as any planted tree
In fair Valencia, never more to roam.
"Good ! good ! most worthy of a great hidalgo !
And Roldan was the man !   But Annibal—
A monkey like no other, though morose
In private character, yet full of tricks—
'Twere hard to carry him, yet harder still
To leave the boy and him in company
And free to slip away.   The boy was wild
And shy as mountain kid ; once hid himself
And tried to run away ; and Annibal,
Who always took the lad's side (he was small,
And they were nearer of a size, and, sirs,
Your monkey has a spite against us men
For being bigger)—Annibal went too.
Would hardly know himself, were he to lose
Both boy and monkey—and 'twas property,
The trouble he had put in Annibal.
He didn't choose another man should beat
His boy and monkey.   If they ran away
Some man would snap them up, and square
       himself

And say they were his goods—he'd taught them
　　　—no !
He Roldan had no mind another man
Should fatten by his monkey, and the boy
Should not be kicked by any pair of sticks
Calling himself a juggler." . . .

　　　　　　　　　　　　But the Duke,
Tired of that hammering, signed that it should
　　　cease ;
Bade Roldan quit all fears—the boy and ape
Should be safe lodged in Abderahman's tower,
In keeping of the great physician there,
The Duke's most special confidant and friend,
One skilled in taming brutes, and always kind.
The Duke himself this eve would see them
　　　lodged.
Roldan must go—spend no more words—but go.

———

The Astrologer's Study.

A room high up in Abderahman's tower,
A window open to the still warm eve,
And the bright disk of royal Jupiter.
Lamps burning low make little atmospheres
Of light amid the dimness ; here and there
Show books and phials, stones and instruments.
In carved dark-oaken chair, unpillowed, sleeps
Right in the rays of Jupiter a small man,
In skull-cap bordered close with crisp gray curls,
And loose black gown showing a neck and breast
Protected by a dim-green amulet ;
Pale-faced, with finest nostril wont to breathe
Ethereal passion in a world of thought ;
Eyebrows jet-black and firm, yet delicate ;

Beard scant and grizzled ; mouth shut firm, with
     curves
So subtly turned to meanings exquisite,
You seem to read them as you read a word
Full-vowelled, long-descended, pregnant—rich
With legacies from long, laborious lives.
Close by him, like a genius of sleep,
Purrs the gray cat, bridling, with snowy breast.
A loud knock.   "Forward !" in clear vocal ring.
Enter the Duke, Pablo, and Annibal.
Exit the cat, retreating toward the dark.

DON SILVA.

You slept, Sephardo.   I am come too soon.

SEPHARDO.

Nay, my lord, it was I who slept too long.
I go to court among the stars to-night,
So bathed my soul beforehand in deep sleep.
But who are these ?

DON SILVA.

     Small guests, for whom I ask
Your hospitality.   Their owner comes
Some short time hence to claim them.   I am
     pledged
To keep them safely ; so I bring them you,
Trusting your friendship for small animals.

SEPHARDO.

Yea, am not I too a small animal ?

DON SILVA.

I shall be much beholden to your love
If you will be their guardian.   I can trust
No other man so well as you.   The boy
Will please you with his singing, touches too
The viol wondrously.

SEPHARDO.

They are welcome both.
Their names are ——?

DON SILVA.

Pablo, this—this Annibal,
And yet, I hope, no warrior.

SEPHARDO.

We'll make peace.
Come, Pablo, let us loosen our friend's chain.
Deign you, my lord, to sit.   Here Pablo, thou—
Close to my chair.   Now Annibal shall choose.

[The cautious monkey, in a Moorish dress,
A tunic white, turban and scimitar,
Wears these stage garments, nay, his very flesh
With silent protest ; keeps a neutral air
As aiming at a metaphysic state
'Twixt " is" and " is not ;" lets his chain be
        loosed
By sage Sephardo's hands, sits still at first,
Then trembles out of his neutrality,
Looks up and leaps into Sephardo's lap,
And chatters forth his agitated soul,
Turning to peep at Pablo on the floor.]

SEPHARDO.

See, he declares we are at amity !

DON SILVA.

No brother sage had read your nature faster.

SEPHARDO.

Why, so he *is* a brother sage.   Man thinks
Brutes have no wisdom, since they know not his :
Can we divine their world ?—the hidden life

That mirrors us as hideous shapeless power,
Cruel supremacy of sharp-edged death,
Or fate that leaves a bleeding mother robbed ?
Oh, they have long tradition and swift speech,
Can tell with touches and sharp darting cries
Whole histories of timid races taught
To breathe in terror by red-handed man.

Don Silva.

Ah, you denounce my sport with hawk and
    hound.
I would not have the angel Gabriel
As hard as you in noting down my sins.

Sephardo.

Nay, they are virtues for you warriors—
Hawking and hunting ! You are merciful
When you leave killing men to kill the brutes.
But, for the point of wisdom, I would choose
To know the mind that stirs between the wings
Of bees and building wasps, or fills the woods
With myriad murmurs of responsive sense
And true-aimed impulse, rather than to know
The thoughts of warriors.

Don Silva.

        Yet they are warriors too—
Your animals. Your judgment limps, Sephardo.
Death is the king of this world ; 'tis his park
Where he breeds life to feed him. Cries of pain
Are music for his banquet ; and the masque—
The last grand masque for his diversion, is
The Holy Inquisition.

Sephardo.

        Ay, anon
I may chime in with you. But not the less

My judgment has firm feet. Though death were
    king,
And cruelty his right-hand minister,
Pity insurgent in some human breasts
Makes spiritual empire, reigns supreme
As persecuted faith in faithful hearts.
Your small physician, weighing ninety pounds,
A petty morsel for a healthy shark,
Will worship mercy throned within his soul,
Though all the luminous angels of the stars
Burst into cruel chorus on his ear,
Singing, '' We know no mercy.'' He would cry
'' I know it'' still, and soothe the frightened bird
And feed the child a-hungered, walk abreast
Of persecuted men, and keep most hate
For rational torturers. There I stand firm.
But you are bitter, and my speech rolls on
Out of your note.

DON SILVA.

       No, no, I follow you.
I too have that within which I will worship
In spite of . . . Yes, Sephardo, I am bitter.
I need your counsel, foresight, all your aid.
Lay these small guests to bed, then we will talk.

SEPHARDO.

See, they are sleeping now. The boy has made
My leg his pillow. For my brother sage,
He'll never heed us ; he knit long ago
A sound ape-system, wherein men are brutes
Emitting doubtful noises. Pray, my lord,
Unlade what burthens you : my ear and hand
Are servants of a heart much bound to you.

DON SILVA.

Yes, yours is love that roots in gifts bestowed
By you on others, and will thrive the more

The more it gives.   I have a double want :
First a confessor—not a Catholic ;
A heart without a livery—naked manhood.

SEPHARDO.

My lord, I will be frank ; there's no such thing
As naked manhood.   If the stars look down
On any mortal of our shape, whose strength
Is to judge all things without preference,
He is a monster, not a faithful man.
While my heart beats, it shall wear livery—
My people's livery, whose yellow badge
Marks them for Christian scorn.   I will not
        say
Man is first man to me, then Jew or Gentile :
That suits the rich *marranos ;* but to me
My father is first father and then man.
So much for frankness' sake.   But let that pass.
'Tis true at least, I am no Catholic
But Salomo Sephardo, a born Jew,
Willing to serve Don Silva.

DON SILVA.

                        Oft you sing
Another strain, and melt distinctions down
As no more real than the wall of dark
Seen by small fishes' eyes, that pierce a span
In the wide ocean.   Now you league yourself
To hem me, hold me prisoner in bonds
Made, say you—how ?—by God or Demiurge,
By spirit or flesh—I care not !   Love was made
Stronger than bonds, and where they press **must**
        break them.
I came to you that I might breathe at large,
And now you stifle me with talk of birth,
Of race and livery.   Yet you knew Fedalma.
She was your friend, Sephardo.   And you know

She is gone from me—know the hounds are
    loosed
To dog me if I seek her.

SEPHARDO.

                Yes, I know.
Forgive me that I used untimely speech,
Pressing a bruise. I loved her well, my lord:
A woman mixed of such fine elements
That were all virtue and religion dead
She'd make them newly, being what she was.

DON SILVA.

Was? say not *was*, Sephardo ! She still lives—
Is, and is mine ; and I will not renounce
What heaven, nay, what she gave me. I will
    sin,
If sin I must, to win my life again.
The fault lie with those powers who have em-
    broiled
The world in hopeless conflict, where all truth
Fights manacled with falsehood, and all good
Makes but one palpitating life with ill.

    (DON SILVA *pauses.* SEPHARDO *is silent.*)

Sephardo, speak ! am I not justified ?
You taught my mind to use the wing that soars
Above the petty fences of the herd :
Now, when I need your doctrine, you are dumb.

SEPHARDO.

Patience ! Hidalgos want interpreters
Of untold dreams and riddles ; they insist
On dateless horoscopes, on formulas
To raise a possible spirit, nowhere named.
Science must be their wishing-cap ; the stars

Speak plainer for high largesse.   No, my lord !
I cannot counsel you to unknown deeds.
This much I can divine : you wish to find
Her whom you love—to make a secret search.

DON SILVA.

That is begun already : a messenger
Unknown to all has been despatched this night.
But forecast must be used, a plan devised,
Ready for service when my scout returns,
Bringing the invisible thread to guide my steps
Toward that lost self my life is aching with.
Sephardo, I will go : and I must go
Unseen by all save you ; though, at our need,
We may trust Alvar.

SEPHARDO.

       A grave task, my lord.
Have you a shapen purpose, or mere will
That sees the end alone and not the means ?
Resolve will melt no rocks.

DON SILVA.

       But it can scale them.
This fortress has two private issues : one,
Which served the Gypsies' flight, to me is
    closed :
Our bands must watch the outlet, now betrayed
To cunning enemies.   Remains one other,
Known to no man save me : a secret left
As heirloom in our house : a secret safe
Even from him—from Father Isidor.
'Tis he who forces me to use it—he :
All's virtue that cheats bloodhounds.   Hear,
    Sephardo.
Given, my scout returns and brings me news

I can straight act on, I shall want your aid.
The issue lies below this tower, your fastness,
Where, by my charter, you rule absolute.
I shall feign illness ; you with mystic air
Must speak of treatment asking vigilance
(Nay I *am* ill—my life has half ebbed out).
I shall be whimsical, devolve command
On Don Diego, speak of poisoning,
Insist on being lodged within this tower.
And rid myself of tendance save from you
And perhaps from Alvar.   So I shall escape
Unseen by spies, shall win the days I need
To ransom her and have her safe enshrined.
No matter, were my flight disclosed at last :
I shall come back as from a duel fought
Which no man can undo.   Now you know all.
Say, can I count on you ?

SEPHARDO.
                    For faithfulness
In aught that I may promise, yes, my lord.
But—for a pledge of faithfulness—this warning.
I will betray nought for your personal harm :
I love you.   But note this—I am a Jew ;
And while the Christian persecutes my race,
I'll turn at need even the Christian's trust
Into a weapon and a shield for Jews.
Shall Cruelty crowned—wielding the savage force
Of multitudes, and calling savageness God
Who gives it victory—upbraid deceit
And ask for faithfulness ?   I love you well.
You are my friend.   But yet you are a Christian,
Whose birth has bound you to the Catholic kings.
There may come moments when to share my joy
Would make you traitor, when to share your
        grief
Would make me other than a Jew . . . .

Don Silva.

                                        What need
To urge that now, Sephardo?   I am one
Of many Spanish nobles who detest
The roaring bigotry of the herd, would fain
Dash from the lips of king and queen the cup
Filled with besotting venom, half infused
By avarice and half by priests.   And now—
Now when the cruelty you flout me with
Pierces me too in the apple of my eye,
Now when my kinship scorches me like hate
Flashed from a mother's eye, you choose this time
To talk of birth as of inherited rage
Deep-down, volcanic, fatal, bursting forth
From   under   hard-taught   reason ?   Wondrous
        friend !
My uncle Isidor's echo, mocking me,
From the opposing quarter of the heavens,
With iteration of the thing I know,
That I'm a Christian knight and Spanish duke !
The consequence ?   Why, that I know.   It lies
In my own hands and not on raven tongues.
The knight and noble shall not wear the chain
Of false-linked thoughts in brains of other men.
What question was there 'twixt us two, of aught
That makes division ?   When I come to you
I come for other doctrine than the Prior's.

Sephardo.

My lord, you are o'erwrought by pain. My words,
That carried innocent meaning, do but float
Like little emptied cups upon the flood
Your mind brings with it.   I but answered you
With regular proviso, such as stands
In testaments and charters, to forefend
A possible case which none deem likelihood ;
Just turned my sleeve, and pointed to the brand

Of brotherhood that limits every pledge.
Superfluous nicety—the student's trick,
Who will not drink until he can define
What water is and is not.   But enough.
My will to serve you now knows no division
Save the alternate beat of love and fear.
There's danger in this quest—name, honor, life—
My lord, the stake is great, and are you
      sure . . .

Don Silva.

No, I am sure of nought but this, Sephardo,
That I will go.   Prudence is but conceit
Hoodwinked by ignorance.   There's nought
      exists
That is not dangerous and holds not death
For souls or bodies.   Prudence turns its helm
To flee the storm and lands 'mid pestilence.
Wisdom would end by throwing dice with folly
But for dire passion which alone makes choice.
And I have chosen as the lion robbed
Chooses to turn upon the ravisher.
If love were slack, the Prior's imperious will
Would move it to outmatch him.   But, Sephardo,
Were all else mute, all passive as sea-calms,
My soul is one great hunger—I must see her.
Now you are smiling.   Oh, you merciful men
Pick up coarse griefs and fling them in the face
Of us whom life with long descent has trained
To subtler pains, mocking your ready balms.
You smile at my soul's hunger.

Sephardo.
                Science smiles
And sways our lips in spite of us, my lord,
When thought weds fact—when maiden prophecy
Waiting, believing, sees the bridal torch.

I use not vulgar measures for your grief,
My pity keeps no cruel feasts ; but thought
Has joys apart, even in blackest woe,
And seizing some fine thread of verity
Knows momentary godhead.

DON SILVA.

And your thought?

SEPHARDO.

Seized on the close agreement of your words
With what is written in your horoscope.

DON SILVA.

Reach it me now.

SEPHARDO.

By your leave, Annibal.

(*He places* ANNIBAL *on* PABLO'S *lap and rises.
The boy moves without waking, and his
head falls on the opposite side.* SEPHARDO
fetches a cushion and lays PABLO'S *head
gently down upon it, then goes to reach the
parchment from a cabinet.* ANNIBAL,
*having waked up in alarm, shuts his eyes
quickly again and pretends to sleep.*)

DON SILVA.

I wish, by new appliance of your skill,
Reading afresh the records of the sky,
You could detect more special augury.
Such chance oft happens, for all characters
Must shrink or widen, as our wine-skins do,
For more or less that we can pour in them ;
And added years give ever a new key
To fixed prediction.

SEPHARDO (*returning with the parchment and reseating himself*).

               True ; our growing thought
Makes growing revelation.   But demand not
Specific augury, as of sure success
In meditated projects, or of ends
To be foreknown by peeping in God's scroll.
I say—nay, Ptolemy said it, but wise books
For half the truths they hold are honored tombs—
Prediction is contingent, of effects
Where causes and concomitants are mixed
To seeming wealth of possibilities
Beyond our reckoning.   Who will pretend
To tell the adventures of each single fish
Within the Syrian Sea ?   Show me a fish,
I'll weigh him, tell his kind, what he devoured,
What would have devoured *him*—but for one Blas
Who netted him instead ; nay, could I tell
That had Blas missed him, he would not have
     died
Of poisonous mud, and so made carrion,
Swept off at last by some sea-scavenger ?

DON SILVA.

Ay, now you talk of fishes, you get hard.
I note you merciful men : you can endure
Torture of fishes and hidalgos.   Follows ?

SEPHARDO.

By how much, then, the fortunes of a man
Are made of elements refined and mixed
Beyond a tunny's, what our science tells
Of the star's influence hath contingency
In special issues.   Thus, the loadstone draws,
Acts like a will to make the iron submiss ;
But garlic rubbing it, that chief effect
Lies in suspense ; the iron keeps at large,

And garlic is controller of the stone.
And so, my lord, your horoscope declares
Not absolutely of your sequent lot,
But, by our lore's authentic rules, sets forth
What gifts, what dispositions, likelihoods
The aspects of the heavens conspired to fuse
With your incorporate soul. Aught more than this
Is vulgar doctrine. For the ambient,
Though a cause regnant, is not absolute,
But suffers a determining restraint
From action of the subject qualities
In proximate motion.

DON SILVA.

　　　　　Yet you smiled just now
At some close fitting of my horoscope
With present fact—with this resolve of mine
To quit the fortress ?

SEPHARDO.

　　　　　Nay, not so ; I smiled,
Observing how the temper of your soul
Sealed long tradition of the influence shed
By the heavenly spheres. Here is your horo-
　　　scope :
The aspects of the Moon with Mars conjunct,
Of Venus and the Sun with Saturn, lord
Of the ascendant, make symbolic speech
Whereto your words gave running paraphrase.

DON SILVA (*impatiently*).

What did I say ?

SEPHARDO.

　　　　　You spoke as oft you did
When I was schooling you at Córdova,
And lessons on the noun and verb were drowned
With sudden stream of general debate

On things and actions.   Always in that stream
I saw the play of babbling currents, saw
A nature o'er-endowed with opposites
Making a self alternate, where each hour
Was critic of the last, each mood too strong
For tolerance of its fellow in close yoke.
The ardent planets stationed as supreme,
Potent in action, suffer light malign
From luminaries large and coldly bright
Inspiring meditative doubt, which straight
Doubts of itself, by interposing act
Of Jupiter in the fourth house fortified
With power ancestral.   So, my lord, I read
The changeless in the changing ; so I read
The constant action of celestial powers
Mixed into waywardness of mortal men,
Whereof no sage's eye can trace the course
And see the close.

DON SILVA.

                    Fruitful result, O sage !
Certain uncertainty.

SEPHARDO.

                    Yea, a result
Fruitful as seeded earth, where certainty
Would be as barren as a globe of gold.
I love you, and would serve you well, my lord.
Your rashness vindicates itself too much,
Puts harness on of cobweb theory
While rushing like a cataract.   Be warned.
Resolve with you is a fire-breathing steed,
But it sees visions, and may feel the air
Impassable with thoughts that come too late,
Rising from out the grave of murdered honor.
Look at your image in your horoscope :

        (*Laying the horoscope before* DON SILVA.)

You are so mixed, my lord, that each to-day
May seem a maniac to its morrow.

DON SILVA (*pushing away the horoscope, rising
and turning to look out at the open window*).

                           No!
No morrow e'er will say that I am mad
Not to renounce her.   Risks !   I know them all.
I've dogged each lurking, ambushed consequence.
I've handled every chance to know its shape
As blind men handle bolts.   Oh, I'm too sane !
I see the Prior's nets.   He does my deed ;
For he has narrowed all my life to this—
That I must find her by some hidden means.

(*He turns and stands close in front of* SEPHARDO.)

One word, Sephardo—leave that horoscope,
Which is but iteration of myself,
And give me promise.   Shall I count on you
To act upon my signal ?   Kings of Spain
Like me have found their refuge in a Jew,
And trusted in his counsel.   You will help me ?

SEPHARDO.

Yes, my lord, I will help you.   Israel
Is to the nations as the body's heart :
Thus writes our poet Jehuda.   I will act
So that no man may ever say through me
" Your Israel is nought," and make my deeds
The mud they fling upon my brethren.
I will not fail you, save—you know the terms :
I am a Jew, and not that infamous life
That takes on bastardy, will know no father,
So shrouds itself in the pale abstract, Man.
You should be sacrificed to Israel
If Israel needed it.

DOŇ SILVA.

I fear not that.
I am no friend of fines and banishment,
Or flames that, fed on heretics, still gape,
And must have heretics made to feed them still.
I take your terms, and for the rest, your love
Will not forsake me.

SEPHARDO.

'Tis hard Roman love,
That looks away and stretches forth the sword
Bared for its master's breast to run upon.
But you will have it so.   Love shall obey.

(DON SILVA *turns to the window again, and
is silent for a few moments, looking at
the sky.*)

DON SILVA.

See now, Sephardo, you would keep no faith
To smooth the path of cruelty.   Confess,
The deed I would not do, save for the strait
Another brings me to (quit my command,
Resign it for brief space, I mean no more)—
Were that deep branded, then the brand should
        fix
On him who urged me.

SEPHARDO.

Will it, though, my lord?

DON SILVA.

I speak not of the fact but of the right.

SEPHARDO.

My lord, you said but now you were resolved.
Question not if the world will be unjust
Branding your deed.   If conscience has two courts

With differing verdicts, where shall lie the appeal?
Our law must be without us or within.
The Highest speaks through all our people's
      voice,
Custom, tradition, and old sanctities ;
Or he reveals himself by new decrees
Of inward certitude.

DON SILVA.

      My love for her
Makes highest law, must be the voice of God.

SEPHARDO.

I thought, but now, you seemed to make excuse,
And plead as in some court where Spanish
      knights
Are tried by other laws than those of love.

DON SILVA.

'Twas momentary.   I shall dare it all.
How the great planet glows, and looks at me,
And seems to pierce me with his effluence !
Were he a living God, these rays that stir
In me the pulse of wonder were in him
Fulness of knowledge.   Are you certified,
Sephardo, that the astral science shrinks
To such pale ashes, dead symbolic forms
For that congenital mixture of effects
Which life declares without the aid of lore?
If there are times propitious or malign
To our first framing, then must all events
Have favoring periods : you cull your plants
By signal of the heavens, then why not trace
As others would by astrologic rule
Times of good augury for momentous acts,—
As secret journeys ?

SEPHARDO.

        Oh, my lord, the stars
Act not as witchcraft or as muttered spells.
I said before they are not absolute,
And tell no fortunes. I adhere alone
To such tradition of their agencies
As reason fortifies.

DON SILVA.

        A barren science !
Some argue now 'tis folly. 'Twere as well
Be of their mind. If those bright stars had will—
But they are fatal fires, and know no love.
Of old, I think, the world was happier
With many gods, who held a struggling life
As mortals do, and helped men in the straits
Of forced misdoing. I doubt that horoscope.

    (DON SILVA *turns from the window and re-
      seats himself opposite* SEPHARDO.)

I am most self-contained, and strong to bear.
No man save you has seen my trembling lip
Utter her name, since she was lost to me.
I'll face the progeny of all my deeds.

SEPHARDO.

May they be fair ! No horoscope makes slaves.
'Tis but a mirror, shows one image forth,
And leaves the future dark with endless " ifs."

DON SILVA.

I marvel, my Sephardo, you can pinch
With confident selection these few grains,
And call them verity, from out the dust
Of crumbling error. Surely such thought creeps,
With insect exploration of the world.
Were I a Hebrew, now, I would be bold.
Why should you fear, not being Catholic ?

SEPHARDO.

Lo ! you yourself, my lord, mix subtleties
With gross belief ; by momentary lapse
Conceive, with all the vulgar, that we Jews
Must hold ourselves God's outlaws, and defy
All good with blasphemy, because we hold
Your good is evil ; think we must turn pale
To see our portraits painted in your hell,
And sin the more for knowing we are lost.

DON SILVA.

Read not my words with malice.   I but meant,
My temper hates an over-cautious march.

SEPHARDO.

The Unnamable made not the search for truth
To suit hidalgos' temper.   I abide
By that wise spirit of listening reverence
Which marks the boldest doctors of our race.
For Truth, to us, is like a living child
Born of two parents : if the parents part
And will divide the child, how shall it live ?
Or, I will rather say : Two angels guide
The path of men, both aged and yet young,
As angels are, ripening through endless years.
On one he leans : some call her Memory,
And some, Tradition ; and her voice is sweet,
With deep mysterious accords : the other,
Floating above, holds down a lamp which streams
A light divine and searching on the earth,
Compelling eyes and footsteps.   Memory yields,
Yet clings with loving check, and shines anew
Reflecting all the rays of that bright lamp
Our angel Reason holds.   We had not walked
But for Tradition ; we walk evermore
To higher paths, by brightening Reason's lamp.

Still we are purblind, tottering.   I hold less
Than Aben-Ezra, of that aged lore
Brought by long centuries from Chaldæan plains ;
The Jew-taught Florentine rejects it all.
For still the light is measured by the eye,
And the weak organ fails.   I may see ill ;
But over all belief is faithfulness,
Which fulfils vision with obedience.
So, I must grasp my morsels : truth is oft
Scattered in fragments round a stately pile
Built half of error ; and the eye's defect
May breed too much denial.   But, my lord,
I weary your sick soul.   Go now with me
Into the turret.   We will watch the spheres,
And see the constellations bend and plunge
Into a depth of being where our eyes
Hold them no more.   We'll quit ourselves and be
The red Aldebaran or bright Sirius,
And sail as in a solemn voyage, bound
On some great quest we know not.

DON SILVA.

                                        Let us go.
She may be watching too, and thought of her
Sways me, as if she knew, to every act
Of pure allegiance.

SEPHARDO.

                    That is love's perfection—
Tuning the soul to all her harmonies
So that no chord can jar.   Now we will mount.

*A large hall in the Castle, of Moorish architecture.
On the side where the windows are, an outer
gallery. Pages and other young gentlemen at-
tached to* DON SILVA'S *household, gathered
chiefly at one end of the hall. Some are moving about ; others are lounging on the carved
benches ; others, half stretched on pieces of
matting and carpet, are gambling.* ARIAS, *a
stripling of fifteen, sings by snatches in a boy-
ish treble, as he walks up and down, and tosses
back the nuts which another youth flings
toward him. In the middle* DON AMADOR,
*a gaunt, gray-haired soldier, in a handsome
uniform, sits in a marble red-cushioned chair,
with a large book spread out on his knees,
from which he is reading aloud, while his
voice is half drowned by the talk that is going
on around him, first one voice and then another surging above the hum.*

ARIAS (*singing*).
*There was a holy hermit
    Who counted all things loss
For Christ his Master's glory :
    He made an ivory cross,
And as he knelt before it
    And wept his murdered Lord,
The ivory turned to iron,
    The cross became a sword.*

JOSÉ (*from the floor*).
I say, twenty cruzados ! thy Galician wit can
never count.

HERNANDO (*also from the floor*).
And thy Sevillian wit always counts double.

ARIAS (*singing*).

The tears that fell upon it,
  They turned to red, red rust,
The tears that fell from off it
  Made writing in the dust.
The holy hermit, gazing,
  Saw words upon the ground :
" *The sword be red forever*
  With the blood of false Mahound."

DON AMADOR (*looking up from his book, and*
raising his voice).

What, gentlemen ! Our Glorious Lady defend
us !

ENRIQUEZ (*from the benches*).

Serves the infidels right ! They have sold
Christians enough to people half the towns in
Paradise. If the Queen, now, had divided the
pretty damsels of Malaga among the Castilians
who have been helping in the holy war, and not
sent half of them to Naples . . .

ARIAS (*singing again*).

At the battle of Clavijo
In the days of King Ramiro,
Help us, Allah ! cried the Moslem,
Cried the Spaniard, Heaven's chosen,
                    God and Santiago !

FABIAN.

Oh, the very tail of our chance has vanished.
The royal army is breaking up—going home for
the winter. The Grand Master sticks to his own
border.

ARIAS (*singing.*)

Straight out-flushing like the rainbow,
See him come, celestial Baron,

Mounted knight, with red-crossed banner,
Plunging earthward to the battle,
                    Glorious Santiago !

HURTADO.

Yes, yes, through the pass of By-and-by, you
go to the valley of Never.   We might have done
a great feat, if the Marquis of Cadiz . . .

ARIAS (*sings*).

As the flame before the swift wind,
See, he fires us, we burn with him !
Flash our swords, dash Pagans backward—
Victory he ! pale fear is Allah !
                    God with Santiago !

DON AMADOR (*raising his voice to a cry*).

Sangre de Dios, gentlemen !

(*He shuts the book, and lets it fall with a bang*
    on the floor.   There is instant silence.)

To what good end is it that I, who studied at
Salamanca, and can write verses agreeable to the
Glorious Lady with the point of a sword which
hath done harder service, am reading aloud in a
clerkly manner from a book which hath been culled
from the flowers of all books, to instruct you in
the knowledge befitting those who would be
knights and worthy hidalgos ?   I had as lief be
reading in a belfry.   And gambling too !   As if
it were a time when we needed not the help of
God and the saints !   Surely for the space of one
hour ye might subdue your tongues to your ears,
that so your tongues might learn somewhat of
civility and modesty.   Wherefore am I master of
the Duke's retinue, if my voice is to run along
like a gutter in a storm ?

HURTADO (*lifting up the book, and respectfully presenting it to* DON AMADOR.

Pardon, Don Amador! The air is so commoved by your voice, that it stirs our tongues in spite of us.

DON AMADOR (*reopening the book*).

Confess, now, it is a goose-headed trick, that when rational sounds are made for your edification, you find nought in it but an occasion for purposeless gabble. I will report it to the Duke, and the reading-time shall be doubled, and my office of reader shall be handed over to Fray Domingo.

(*While* DON AMADOR *has been speaking,* DON SILVA, *with* DON ALVAR, *has appeared walking in the outer gallery on which the windows are opened.*)

ALL (*in concert*).

No, no, no.

DON AMADOR.

Are ye ready, then, to listen, if I finish the wholesome extract from the Seven Parts, wherein the wise King Alfonso hath set down the reason why knights should be of gentle birth? Will ye now be silent?

ALL.

Yes, silent.

DON AMADOR.

But when I pause, and look up, I give any leave to speak, if he hath aught pertinent to say.

(Reads.)

" And this nobility cometh in three ways : *first*, by lineage, *secondly*, by science, and *thirdly*, by valor and worthy behavior. Now, although they who gain nobility through science or good deeds are rightfully called noble and gentle ; nevertheless, they are with the highest fitness so called who are noble by ancient lineage, and lead a worthy life as by inheritance from afar ; and hence are more bound and constrained to act well, and guard themselves from error and wrong-doing ; for in their case it is more true that by evil-doing they bring injury and shame not only on themselves, but also on those from whom they are derived."

DON AMADOR (*placing his forefinger for a mark on the page, and looking up, while he keeps his voice raised, as wishing* DON SILVA *to overhear him in the judicious discharge of his function.*)

Hear ye that, young gentlemen ? See ye not that if ye have but bad manners even, they disgrace you more than gross misdoings disgrace the low-born ? Think you, Arias, it becomes the son of your house irreverently to sing and fling nuts, to the interruption of your elders ?

ARIAS (*sitting on the floor, and leaning backward on his elbows*).

Nay, Don Amador ; King Alfonso, they say, was a heretic, and I think that is not true writing. For noble birth gives us more leave to do ill if we like.

DON AMADOR (*lifting his brows*).

What bold and blasphemous talk is this ?

ARIAS.

Why, nobles are only punished now and then,
in a grand way, and have their heads cut off, like
the Grand Constable.   I shouldn't mind that.

JOSÉ.

Nonsense, Arias! nobles have their heads cut
off because their crimes are noble.   If they did
what was unknightly, they would come to shame.
Is not that true, Don Amador?

DON AMADOR.

Arias is a contumacious puppy, who will bring
dishonor on his parentage.   Pray, sirrah, whom
did you ever hear speak as you have spoken?

ARIAS.

Nay, I speak out of my own head.   I shall go
and ask the Duke.

HURTADO.

Now, now! you are too bold, Arias.

ARIAS.

Oh, he is never angry with me,—(*Dropping his
voice*) because the Lady Fedalma liked me.   She
said I was a good boy, and pretty, and that is what
you are not, Hurtado.

HURTADO.

Girl-face!   See, now, if you dare ask the Duke.

(DON SILVA *is just entering the hall from
the gallery, with* DON ALVAR *behind
him, intending to pass out at the other
end.   All rise with homage.* DON
SILVA *bows coldly and abstractedly.*
ARIAS *advances from the group, and
goes up to* DON SILVA.)

ARIAS.

My lord, is it true that a noble is more dishonored than other men if he does aught dishonor-
able ?

DON SILVA (*first blushing deeply, and grasping
his sword, then raising his hand and giving
ARIAS a blow on the ear*).

Varlet !

ARIAS.

My lord, I am a gentleman.

(DON SILVA *pushes him away, and passes on
hurriedly.*)

DON ALVAR (*following and turning to speak*).

Go, go ! you should not speak to the Duke
when you are not called upon. He is ill and
much distempered.

(ARIAS *retires, flushed, with tears in his eyes.
His companions look too much sur-
prised to triumph.* DON AMADOR *remains silent and confused.*)

------

*The Plaça Santiago during busy market-time.
Mules and asses laden with fruits and vege-
tables. Stalls and booths filled with wares of
all sorts. A crowd of buyers and sellers. A
stalwart woman, with keen eyes, leaning over
the panniers of a mule laden with apples,
watches* LORENZO, *who is lounging through
the market. As he approaches her, he is met
by* BLASCO.

LORENZO.

Well met, friend.

BLASCO.

     Ay, for we are soon to.part,
And I would see you at the hostelry,
To take my reckoning. I go forth to-day.

LORENZO.

'Tis grievous parting with good company.
I would I had the gold to pay such guests
For all my pleasure in their talk.

BLASCO.

        Why, yes ;
A solid-headed man of Aragon
Has matter in him that you Southerners lack.
You like my company—'tis natural.
But, look you, I have done my business well,
Have sold and ta'en commissions. I come
   straight
From—you know who—I like not naming him.
I'm a thick man : you reach not my backbone
With any tooth-pick ; but I tell you this :
He reached it with his eye, right to the marrow.
It gave me heart that I had plate to sell,
For, saint or no saint, a good silversmith
Is wanted for God's service ; and my plate—
He judged it well—bought nobly.

LORENZO.

       A great man,
And holy !

BLASCO.

   Yes, I'm glad I leave to-day.
For there are stories give a sort of smell—
One's nose has fancies. A good trader, sir,
Likes not this plague of lapsing in the air,
Most caught by men with funds. And they *do* say

There's a great terror here in Moors and Jews,
I would say, Christians of unhappy blood.
'Tis monstrous, sure, that men of substance lapse,
And risk their property.   I know I'm sound.
No heresy was ever bait to me.   Whate'er
Is the right faith, that I believe—nought else.

LORENZO.

Ay, truly, for the flavor of true faith
Once known must sure be sweetest to the taste.
But an uneasy mood is now abroad
Within the town ; partly, for that the Duke
Being sorely sick, has yielded the command
To Don Diego, a most valiant man,
More Catholic than the Holy Father's self,
Half chiding God that He will tolerate
A Jew or Arab ; though 'tis plain they're made
For profit of good Christians.   And weak heads—
Panic will knit all disconnected facts—
Draw hence belief in evil auguries,
Rumors of accusation and arrest,
All air-begotten.   Sir, you need not go.
But if it must be so, I'll follow you
In fifteen minutes—finish marketing,
Then be at home to speed you on your way.

BLASCO.

Do so.   I'll back to Saragossa straight.
The court and nobles are retiring now
And wending northward.   There'll be fresh
        demand
For bells and images against the Spring,
When doubtless our great Catholic sovereigns
Will move to conquest of these eastern parts,
And cleanse Granada from the infidel.
Stay, sir, with God, until we meet again !

LORENZO.

Go, sir, with God, until I follow you !

> (*Exit* BLASCO. LORENZO *passes on toward the market-woman, who, as he approaches, raises herself from her leaning attitude.*)

LORENZO.

Good day, my mistress. How's your merchan-
    dise?
Fit for a host to buy? Your apples now,
They have fair cheeks ; how are they at the core?

MARKET-WOMAN.

Good, good, sir ! Taste and try. See, here is one
Weighs a man's head. The best are bound with
    tow :
They're worth the pains, to keep the peel from
    splits.

> (*She takes out an apple bound with tow, and, as she puts it into* LORENZO'S *hand, speaks in a lower tone.*)

'Tis called the Miracle. You open it,
And find it full of speech.

LORENZO.

                  Ay, give it me,
I'll take it to the Doctor in the tower.
He feeds on fruit, and if he likes the sort
I'll buy them for him. Meanwhile, drive your ass
Round to my hostelry. I'll straight be there.
You'll not refuse some barter?

MARKET-WOMAN.

                  No, not I.
Feathers and skins.

LORENZO.

      Good, till we meet again.

(LORENZO, *after smelling at the apple, puts
it into a pouch-like basket which hangs
before him, and walks away. The
woman drives off the mule.*)

———

A LETTER.

" Zarca, the chieftain of the Gypsies, greets
The King El Zagal.   Let the force be sent
With utmost swiftness to the Pass of Luz.
A good five hundred added to my bands
Will master all the garrison : the town
Is half with us, and will not lift an arm
Save on our side.   My scouts have found a way
Where once we thought the fortress most secure :
Spying a man upon the height, they traced,
By keen conjecture piecing broken sight,
His downward path, and found its issue.   There
A file of us can mount, surprise the fort
And give the signal to our friends within
To ope the gates for our confederate bands
Who will lie eastward ambushed by the rocks,
Waiting the night.   Enough ; give me command,
Bedmár is yours.   Chief Zarca will redeem
His pledge of highest service to the Moor :
Let the Moor too be faithful and repay
The Gypsy with the furtherance he needs
To lead his people over Bahr el Scham
And plant them on the shore of Africa.
So may the King El Zagal live as one
Who, trusting Allah will be true to him,
Maketh himself as Allah true to friends."

BOOK III.

QUIT now the town, and with a journeying dream
Swift as the wings of sound yet seeming slow
Through multitudinous pulsing of stored sense
And spiritual space, see walls and towers
Lie in the silent whiteness of a trance,
Giving no sign of that warm life within
That moves and murmurs through their hidden
    heart.
Pass o'er the mountain, wind in sombre shade,
Then wind into the light and see the town
Shrunk to white crust upon the darker rock.
Turn east and south, descend, then rise anew
'Mid smaller mountains ebbing toward the plain :
Scent the fresh breath of the height-loving herbs
That, trodden by the pretty parted hoofs
Of nimble goats, sigh at the innocent bruise,
And with a mingled difference exquisite
Pour a sweet burthen on the buoyant air.
Pause now and be all ear.   Far from the south,
Seeking the listening silence of the heights,
Comes a slow-dying sound—the Moslems' call
To prayer in afternoon.   Bright in the sun
Like tall white sails on a green shadowy sea
Stand Moorish watch-towers : 'neath that eastern
    sky
Couches unseen the strength of Moorish Baza ;
Where the meridian bends lies Guadix, hold
Of brave El Zagal.   This is Moorish land,
Where Allah lives unconquered in dark breasts

And blesses still the many-nourishing earth
With dark-armed industry.   See from the steep
The scattered olives hurry in gray throngs
Down toward the valley, where the little stream
Parts a green hollow 'twixt the gentler slopes ;
And in that hollow, dwellings : not white homes
Of building Moors, but little swarthy tents
Such as of old perhaps on Asian plains,
Or wending westward past the Caucasus,
Our fathers raised to rest in.   Close they swarm
About two taller tents, and viewed afar
Might seem a dark-robed crowd in penitence
That silent kneel ; but come now in their midst
And watch a busy, bright-eyed, sportive life !
Tall maidens been to feed the tethered goat,
The ragged kirtle fringing at the knee
Above the living curves, the shoulder's smooth-
      ness
Parting the torrent strong of ebon hair.
Women with babes, the wild and neutral glance
Swayed now to sweet desire of mothers' eyes,
Rock their strong cradling arms and chant low
      strains
Taught by monotonous and soothing winds
That fall at night-time on the dozing ear.
The crones plait reeds, or shred the vivid herbs
Into the caldron : tiny urchins crawl
Or sit and gurgle forth their infant joy.
Lads lying sphynx-like with uplifted breast
Propped on their elbows, their black manes tossed
      back,
Fling up the coin and watch its fatal fall,
Dispute and scramble, run and wrestle fierce,
Then fall to play and fellowship again ;
Or in a thieving swarm they run to plague
The grandsires, who return with rabbits slung,
And with the mules fruit-laden from the fields.

Some striplings choose the smooth stones from the
     brook
To serve the slingers, cut the twigs for snares,
Or trim the hazel-wands, or at the bark
Of some exploring dog they dart away
With swift precision toward a moving speck.
These are the brood of Zarca's Gypsy tribe ;
Most like an earth-born race bred by the Sun
On some rich tropic soil, the father's light
Flashing in coal-black eyes, the mother's blood
With bounteous elements feeding their young
     limbs.
The stalwart men and youths are at the wars
Following their chief, all save a trusty band
Who keep strict watch along the northern heights.

But see, upon a pleasant spot removed
From the camp's hubbub, where the thicket strong
Of huge-eared cactus makes a bordering curve
And casts a shadow, lies a sleeping man
With Spanish hat screening his upturned face,
His doublet loose, his right arm backward flung,
His left caressing close the long-necked lute
That seems to sleep too, leaning tow'rd its lord.
He draws deep breath secure but not unwatched.
Moving a-tiptoe, silent as the elves,
As mischievous too, trip three bare-footed girls
Not opened yet to womanhood—dark flowers
In slim long buds : some paces farther off
Gathers a little white-teethed shaggy group,
A grinning chorus to the merry play.
The tripping girls have robbed the sleeping man
Of all his ornaments.   Hita is decked
With an embroidered scarf across her rags ;
Tralla, with thorns for pins, sticks two rosettes
Upon her threadbare woollen ; Hinda now,
Prettiest and boldest, tucks her kirtle up

As wallet for the stolen buttons—then
Bends with her knife to cut from off the hat
The aigrette and long feather ; deftly cuts,
Yet wakes the sleeper, who with sudden start
Shakes off the masking hat and shows the face
Of Juan : Hinda swift as thought leaps back,
But carries off the spoil triumphantly,
And leads the chorus of a happy laugh,
Running with all the naked-footed imps,
Till with safe survey all can face about
And watch for signs of stimulating chase,
While Hinda ties long grass around her brow
To stick the feather in with majesty.
Juan still sits contemplative, with looks
Alternate at the spoilers and their work.

JUAN.

Ah, you marauding kite—my feather gone !
My belt, my scarf, my buttons and rosettes !
This is to be a brother of your tribe !
The fiery-blooded children of the Sun—
So says chief Zarca—children of the Sun !
Ay, ay, the black and stinging flies he breeds
To plague the decent body of mankind.
"Orpheus, professor of the *gai saber*,
Made all the brutes polite by dint of song."
Pregnant—but as a guide in daily life
Delusive.   For if song and music cure
The barbarous trick of thieving, 'tis a cure
That works as slowly as old Doctor Time
In curing folly.   Why, the minxes there
Have rhythm in their toes, and music rings
As readily from them as from little bells
Swung by the breeze.   Well, I will try the physic.

(He touches his lute.)

Hem ! taken rightly, any single thing,
The Rabbis say, implies all other things.

A knotty task, though, the unravelling
Meum and *Tuum* from a saraband :
It needs a subtle logic, nay, perhaps
A good large property, to see the thread.

> (*He touches the lute again.*)

There's more of odd than even in this world.
Else pretty sinners would not be let off
Sooner than ugly ; for if honeycombs
Are to be got by stealing, they should go
Where life is bitterest on the tongue. And yet—
Because this minx has pretty ways I wink
At all her tricks, though if a flat-faced lass,
With eyes askew, were half as bold as she,
I should chastise her with a hazel switch.
I'm a plucked peacock—even my voice and wit
Without a tail !—why, any fool detects
The absence of your tail, but twenty fools
May not detect the presence of your wit.

> (*He touches his lute again.*)

Well, I must coax my tail back cunningly,
For to run after these brown lizards—ah !
I think the lizards lift their ears at this.

> (*As he thrums his lute the lads and girls
> gradually approach : he touches it more
> briskly, and* HINDA, *advancing, begins
> to move arms and legs with an initiatory
> dancing movement, smiling coaxingly
> at* JUAN. *He suddenly stops, lays
> down his lute and folds his arms.*)

JUAN.

What, you expect a tune to dance to, eh ?

HINDA, HITA, TRALLA, AND THE REST
(*clapping their hands*).

Yes, yes, a tune, a tune !

JUAN.

But that is what you cannot have, my sweet brothers and sisters. The tunes are all dead— dead as the tunes of the lark when you have plucked his wings off ; dead as the song of the grasshopper when the ass has swallowed him. I can play and sing no more. Hinda has killed my tunes.

> (*All cry out in consternation.* HINDA *gives a wail and tries to examine the lute.*)

JUAN (*waving her off*).

Understand, Señora Hinda, that the tunes are in me ; they are not in the lute till I put them there. And if you cross my humor, I shall be as tuneless as a bag of wool. If the tunes are to be brought to life again, I must have my feather back.

> (HINDA *kisses his hands and feet coaxingly.*)

No, no ! not a note will come for coaxing. The feather, I say, the feather !

> (HINDA *sorrowfully takes off the feather, and gives it to* JUAN.)

Ah, now let us see. Perhaps a tune will come.

> (*He plays a measure, and the three girls begin to dance ; then he suddenly stops.*)

JUAN.

No, the tune will not come : it wants the aigrette (*pointing to it on Hinda's neck*).

> (HINDA, *with rather less hesitation, but again sorrowfully, takes off the aigrette, and gives it to him.*)

JUAN.

Ha ! (*He plays again, but, after rather a longer time, again stops.*) No, no ; 'tis the buttons are wanting, Hinda, the buttons. This tune feeds chiefly on buttons—a greedy tune. It wants one, two, three, four, five, six. Good !

> (*After* HINDA *has given up the buttons, and* JUAN *has laid them down one by one, he begins to play again, going on longer than before, so that the dancers become excited by the movement. Then he stops.*)

JUAN.

Ah, Hita, it is the belt, and, Tralla, the rosettes —both are wanting. I see the tune will not go on without them.

> (HITA *and* TRALLA *take off the belt and rosettes, and lay them down quickly, being fired by the dancing, and eager for the music. All the articles lie by* JUAN'S *side on the ground.*)

JUAN.

Good, good, my docile wild-cats ! Now I think the tunes are all alive again. Now you may dance and sing too. Hinda, my little screamer, lead off with the song I taught you, and let us see if the tune will go right on from beginning to end.

> (*He plays. The dance begins again,* HINDA *singing. All the other boys and girls join in the chorus, and all at last dance wildly.*)

SONG.

All things journey : sun and moon,
Morning, noon, and afternoon,
    Night and all her stars :
"Twixt the east and western bars
    Round they journey,
            Come and go !
    We go with them !
For to roam and ever roam
Is the Zíncali's loved home.

Earth is good, the hillside breaks
By the ashen roots and makes
    Hungry nostrils glad :
Then we run till we are mad,
    Like the horses,
            And we cry,
    None shall catch us !
Swift winds wing us—we are free—
Drink the air—we Zíncali !

Falls the snow : the pine-branch split,
Call the fire out, see it flit,
    Through the dry leaves run,
Spread and glow, and make a sun
    In the dark tent :
            O warm dark !
    Warm as conies !
Strong fire loves us, we are warm !
Who the Zíncali shall harm ?

Onward journey : fires are spent ;
Sunward, sunward ! lift the tent,
    Run before the rain,
Through the pass, along the plain.

Hurry, hurry,
      Lift us, wind!
Like the horses.
For to roam and ever roam
Is the Zíncali's loved home.

(*When the dance is at its height,* HINDA
      *breaks away from the rest, and dances
      round* JUAN, *who is now standing. As
      he turns a little to watch her movement,
      some of the boys skip toward the feather,
      aigrette, etc., snatch them up, and run
      away, swiftly followed by* HITA, TRAL-
      LA, *and the rest.* HINDA, *as she turns
      again, sees them, screams, and falls in
      her whirling; but immediately gets up,
      and rushes after them, still screaming
      with rage.*)

JUAN.

Santiago! these imps get bolder. Haha! Señora Hinda, this finishes your lesson in ethics.
You have seen the advantage of giving up stolen
goods. Now you see the ugliness of thieving
when practised by others. That fable of mine
about the tunes was excellently devised. I feel
like an ancient sage instructing our lisping ancestors. My memory will descend as the Orpheus
of Gypsies. But I must prepare a rod for those
rascals. I'll bastinado them with prickly pears.
It seems to me these needles will have a sound
moral teaching in them.

(*While* JUAN *takes a knife from his belt,
      and surveys a bush of the prickly pear,*
      HINDA *returns.*)

JUAN.

Pray, Señora, why do you fume ? Did you
want to steal my ornaments again yourself ?

HINDA (*sobbing*).

No ; I thought you would give them me back
again.

JUAN.

What, did you want the tunes to die again
Do you like finery better than dancing ?

HINDA.

Oh, that was a tale ! I shall tell tales too,
when I want to get anything I can't steal. And
I know what I will do. I shall tell the boys I've
found some little foxes, and I will never say
where they are till they give me back the feather !

(*She runs off again.*)

JUAN.

Hem ! the disciple seems to seize the mode
sooner than the matter. Teaching virtue with this
prickly pear may only teach the youngsters to use
a new weapon ; as your teaching orthodoxy with
fagots may only bring up a fashion of roasting.
Dios ! my remarks grow too pregnant—my wits
get a plethora by solitary feeding on the produce
of my own wisdom.

(*As he puts up his knife again,* HINDA
*comes running back, and crying, "Our
Queen ! our Queen !"* JUAN *adjusts
his garments and his lute, while* HINDA
turns to meet FEDALMA, *who wears a
Moorish dress, her dark hair hanging
round her in plaits, a white turban on
her head, a dagger by her side. She
carries a scarf on her left arm, which
she holds up as a shade.*)

FEDALMA (*patting* HINDA'S *head*).

How now, wild one? You are hot and panting. Go to my tent, and help Nouna to plait
reeds.

> (HINDA *kisses* FEDALMA'S *hand, and runs
> off.* FEDALMA *advances toward* JUAN,
> *who kneels to take up the edge of her cy-
> mar, and kisses it.*)

JUAN.   ·

How is it with you, lady? You look sad.

FEDALMA.

Oh, I am sick at heart.   The eye of day,
The insistent summer sun, seems pitiless,
Shining in all the barren crevices
Of weary life, leaving no shade, no dark,
Where I may dream that hidden waters lie ;
As pitiless as to some shipwrecked man,
Who gazing from his narrow shoal of sand
On the wide unspecked round of blue and blue
Sees that full light is errorless despair.
The insects' hum that slurs the silent dark
Startles and seems to cheat me, as the tread
Of coming footsteps cheats the midnight watcher
Who holds her heart and waits to hear them
        pause,
And hears them never pause, but pass and die.
Music sweeps by me as a messenger
Carrying a message that is not for me.
The very sameness of the hills and sky
Is obduracy, and the lingering hours
Wait round me dumbly, like superfluous slaves,
Of whom I want nought but the secret news
They are forbid to tell.   And, Juan, you—
You, too, are cruel—would be over-wise

In judging your friend's needs, and choose to
    hide
Something I crave to know.

JUAN.

                I, lady?

FEDALMA.

                      You.

JUAN.

I never had the virtue to hide aught,
Save what a man is whipped for publishing.
I'm no more reticent than the voluble air—
Dote on disclosure—never could contain
The latter half of all my sentences,
But for the need to utter the beginning.
My lust to tell is so importunate
That it abridges every other vice,
And makes me temperate for want of time.
I dull sensation in the haste to say
'Tis this or that, and choke report with surmise.
Judge, then, dear lady, if I could be mute
When but a glance of yours had bid me speak.

FEDALMA.

Nay, sing such falsities !—you mock me worse
By speech that gravely seems to ask belief.
You are but babbling in a part you play
To please my father. Oh, 'tis well meant, say
    you—
Pity for woman's weakness.   Take my thanks.

JUAN.

Thanks angrily bestowed are red-hot coin
Burning your servant's palm.

FEDALMA.

                Deny it not,
You know how many leagues this camp of ours

Lies from Bedmár — what mountains lie be-
    tween—
Could tell me if you would about the Duke—
That he is comforted, sees how he gains
Losing the Zincala, finds now how slight
The thread Fedalma made in that rich web,
A Spanish noble's life.   No, that is false !
He never would think lightly of our love.
Some evil has befallen him—he's slain—
Has sought for danger and has beckoned death
Because I made all life seem treachery.
Tell me the worst—be merciful—no worst,
Against the hideous painting of my fear,
Would not show like a better.

JUAN.

                If I speak,
Will you believe your slave ? For truth is
    scant ;
And where the appetite is still to hear
And not believe, falsehood would stint it less.
How say you ? Does your hunger's fancy choose
The meagre fact ?

    FEDALMA (*seating herself on the ground*).

             Yes, yes, the truth, dear Juan.
Sit now, and tell me all.

JUAN.

              That all is nought.
I can unleash my fancy if you wish
And hunt for phantoms : shoot an airy guess
And bring down airy likelihood—some lie
Masked cunningly to look like royal truth
And cheat the shooter, while King Fact goes
    free ;
Or else some image of reality
That doubt will handle and reject as false.

As for conjecture—I can thread the sky
Like any swallow, but, if you insist
On knowledge that would guide a pair of feet
Right to Bedmár, across the Moorish bounds,
A mule that dreams of stumbling over stones
Is better stored.

FEDALMA.

       And you have gathered nought
About the border wars?   No news, no hint
Of any rumors that concern the Duke—
Rumors kept from me by my father?

JUAN.

           None.
Your father trusts no secret to the echoes.
Of late his movements have been hid from all
Save those few hundred chosen Gypsy breasts
He carries with him.   Think you he's a man
To let his projects slip from out his belt,
Then whisper him who haps to find them strayed
To be so kind as keep his counsel well?
Why, if he found me knowing aught too much,
He would straight gag or strangle me, and say,
"Poor hound! it was a pity that his bark
Could chance to mar my plans : he loved my
      daughter—
The idle hound had nought to do but love,
So followed to the battle and got crushed."

FEDALMA (*holding out her hand, which* JUAN
        kisses).

Good Juan, I could have no nobler friend.
You'd ope your veins and let your life-blood out
To save another's pain, yet hide the deed
With jesting—say, 'twas merest accident,
A sportive scratch that went by chance too deep—

And die content with men's slight thoughts of
    you,
Finding your glory in another's joy.

JUAN.

Dub not my likings virtues, lest they get
A drug-like taste, and breed a nausea.
Honey's not sweet, commended as cathartic.
Such names are parchment labels upon gems
Hiding their color.   What is lovely seen
Priced in a tariff ?—lapis lazuli,
Such bulk, so many drachmas : amethysts
Quoted at so much ; sapphires higher still.
The stone like solid heaven in its blueness
Is what I care for, not its name or price.
So, if I live or die to serve my friend,
'Tis for my love—'tis for my friend alone,
And not for any rate that friendship bears
In heaven or on earth.   Nay, I romance—
I talk of Roland and the ancient peers.
In me 'tis hardly friendship, only lack
Of a substantial self that holds a weight ;
So I kiss larger things and roll with them.

FEDALMA.

Oh, you will never hide your soul from me ;
I've seen the jewel's flash, and know 'tis there,
Muffle it as you will.   That foam-like talk
Will not wash out a fear which blots the good
Your presence brings me.   Oft I'm pierced afresh
Through all the pressure of my selfish griefs
By thought of you.   It was a rash resolve
Made you disclose yourself when you kept watch
About the terrace wall :—your pity leaped,
Seeing alone my ills and not your loss,
Self-doomed to exile.   Juan, you must repent.
'Tis not in nature that resolve, which feeds

On strenuous actions, should not pine and die
In these long days of empty listlessness.

JUAN.

Repent? Not I. Repentance is the weight
Of indigested meals ta'en yesterday.
'Tis for large animals that gorge on prey,
Not for a honey-sipping butterfly.
I am a thing of rhythm and redondillas—
The momentary rainbow on the spray
Made by the thundering torrent of men's lives :
No matter whether I am here or there ;
I still catch sunbeams.   And in Africa,
Where melons and all fruits, they say, grow large,
Fables are real, and the apes polite,
A poet, too, may prosper past belief :
I shall grow epic, like the Florentine,
And sing the founding of our infant state,
Sing the new Gypsy Carthage.

FEDALMA.
Africa
Would we were there !   Under another heaven,
In lands where neither love nor memory
Can plant a selfish hope—in lands so far
I should not seem to see the outstretched arms
That seek me, or to hear the voice that calls.
I should feel distance only and despair ;
So rest forever from the thought of bliss,
And wear my weight of life's great chain un-
        struggling.
Juan, if I could know he would forget—
Nay, not forget, forgive me—be content
That I forsook him for no joy, but sorrow,
For sorrow chosen rather than a joy
That destiny made base !   Then he would taste
No bitterness in sweet, sad memory,

And I should live unblemished in his thought,
Hallowed like her who dies an unwed bride.
Our words have wings, but fly not where we would.
Could mine but reach him, Juan !

JUAN.
Speak the wish—
My feet have wings—I'll be your Mercury.
I fear no shadowed perils by the way.
No man will wear the sharpness of his sword
On me. Nay, I'm a herald of the Muse,
Sacred for Moors and Spaniards. I will go—
Will fetch you tidings for an amulet.
But stretch not hope too strongly toward that
      mark
As issue of my wandering. Given, I cross
Safely the Moorish border, reach Bedmár :
Fresh counsels may prevail there, and the Duke
Being absent in the field, I may be trapped.
Men who are sour at missing larger game
May wing a chattering sparrow for revenge.
It is a chance no further worth the note
Than as a warning, lest you feared worse ill
If my return were stayed. I might be caged ;
They would not harm me else. Untimely death,
The red auxiliary of the skeleton,
Has too much work on hand to think of me ;
Or, if he cares to slay me, I shall fall
Choked with a grape-stone for economy.
The likelier chance is that I go and come,
Bringing you comfort back.

FEDALMA (*starts from her seat and walks to a
    little distance, standing a few moments with her
    back toward* JUAN, *then she turns round quickly,
    and goes toward him*).

No, Juan, no !
Those yearning words came from a soul infirm

Crying and struggling at the pain of bonds
Which yet it would not loosen. He knows all—
All that he needs to know : I said farewell :
I stepped across the cracking earth and knew
'Twould yawn behind me.   I must walk right on.
No, I will not win aught by risking you :
That risk would poison my poor hope.   Besides,
'Twere treachery in me : my father wills
That we—all here—should rest within this camp.
If I can never live, like him, on faith
In glorious morrows, I am resolute.
While he treads painfully with stillest step
And beady brow, pressed 'neath the weight of
      arms,
Shall I, to ease my fevered restlessness,
Raise peevish moans, shattering that fragile
      silence ?
No ! On the close-thronged spaces of the earth
A battle rages : Fate has carried me
'Mid the thick arrows : I will keep my stand—
Not shrink and let the shaft pass by my breast
To pierce another.   Oh, 'tis written large
The thing I have to do.   But you, dear Juan,
Renounce, endure, are brave, unurged by aught
Save the sweet overflow of your good will.

             (She seats herself again.)

JUAN.

Nay, I endure nought worse than napping sheep
When nimble birds uproot a fleecy lock
To line their nest with. See ! your bondsman,
      Queen,
The minstrel of your court, is featherless ;
Deforms your presence by a moulting garb ;
Shows like a roadside bush culled of its buds.
Yet, if your graciousness will not disdain
A poor plucked songster—shall he sing to you ?

Some lay of afternoons—some ballad strain
Of those who ached once but are sleeping now
Under the sun-warmed flowers ?   'Twill cheat the
    time.

FEDALMA.

Thanks, Juan—later, when this hour is passed.
My soul is clogged with self ; it could not float
On with the pleasing sadness of your song.
Leave me in this green spot, but come again,—
Come with the lengthening shadows.

JUAN.

                        Then your slave
Will go to chase the robbers.   Queen, farewell !

FEDALMA.

Best friend, my well-spring in the wilderness !

[While Juan sped along the stream, there came
From the dark tents a ringing joyous shout
That thrilled Fedalma with a summons grave
Yet welcome, too.   Straightway she rose and
    stood,
All languor banished, with a soul suspense,
Like one who waits high presence, listening.
Was it a message, or her father's self
That made the camp so glad?
                        It was himself !
She saw him now advancing, girt with arms
That seemed like idle trophies hung for show
Beside the weight and fire of living strength
That made his frame.   He glanced with absent
    triumph,
As one who conquers in some field afar
And bears off unseen spoil.   But nearing her,
His terrible eyes intense sent forth new rays—
A sudden sunshine where the lightning was
'Twixt meeting dark.   All tenderly he laid

His hand upon her shoulder ; tenderly
His kiss upon her brow.]

ZARCA.

My royal daughter !

FEDALMA.

Father, I joy to see your safe return.

ZARCA.

Nay, I but stole the time, as hungry men
Steal from the morrow's meal, made a forced
    march,
Left Hassan as my watchdog, all to see
My daughter, and to feed her famished hope
With news of promise.

FEDALMA.

Is the task achieved
That was to be the herald of our flight ?

ZARCA.

Not outwardly, but to my inward vision
Things are achieved when they are well begun.
The perfect archer calls the deer his own
While yet the shaft is whistling.   His keen eye
Never sees failure, sees the mark alone.
You have heard nought, then—had no messenger ?

FEDALMA.

I, father? no : each quiet day has fled
Like the same moth, returning with slow wing,
And pausing in the sunshine.

ZARCA.

It is well.
You shall not long count days in weariness.
Ere the full moon has waned again to new,
We shall reach Almeria : Berber ships

Will take us for their freight, and we shall go
With plenteous spoil, not stolen, bravely won
By service done on Spaniards.   Do you shrink?
Are you aught less than a true Zíncala?

FEDALMA.

No ; but I am more.   The Spaniards fostered
    me.

ZARCA.

They stole you first, and reared you for the
    flames.
I found you, rescued you, that you might live
A Zíncala's life ; I saved you from their doom.
Your bridal bed had been the rack.

FEDALMA (*in a low tone*).

                  They meant—
To seize me ?—ere he came ?

ZARCA.

              Yes, I know all.
They found your chamber empty.

FEDALMA (*eagerly*).

              Then you know—
(*checking herself.*)
Father, my soul would be less laggard, fed
With fuller trust.

ZARCA.

            My daugnter, I must keep
The Arab's secret.   Arabs are our friends,
Grappling for life with Christians who lay waste
Granáda's valleys, and with devilish hoofs
Trample the young green corn, with devilish play
Fell blossomed trees, and tear up well-pruned
    vines :

Cruel as tigers to the vanquished brave,
They wring out gold by oaths they mean to
    break ;
Take pay for pity and are pitiless ;
Then tinkle bells above the desolate earth
And praise their monstrous gods, supposed to
    love
The flattery of liars.   I will strike
The full-gorged dragon.   You, my child, must
    watch
The battle with a heart, not fluttering
But duteous, firm-weighted by resolve,
Choosing between two lives, like her who holds
A dagger which must pierce one of two breasts,
And one of them her father's.   You divine—
I speak not closely, but in parables ;
Put one for many.

> FEDALMA (*collecting herself and looking firmly
> at* ZARCA).

            Then it is your will
That I ask nothing ?

> ZARCA.

            You shall know enough
To trace the sequence of the seed and flower.
El Zagal trusts me, rates my counsel high :
He, knowing I have won a grant of lands
Within the Berber's realm, wills me to be
The tongue of his good cause in Africa,
So gives us furtherance in our pilgrimage
For service hoped, as well as service done
In that great feat of which I am the eye,
And my five hundred Gypsies the best arm.
More, I am charged by other noble Moors
With messages of weight to Telemsán.
Ha, your eye flashes.   Are you glad ?

FEDALMA.

Yes, glad
That men can greatly trust a Zincalo.

ZARCA.

Why, fighting for dear life men choose their
    swords
For cutting only, not for ornament.
What nought but Nature gives, man takes per-
    force
Where she bestows it, though in vilest place.
Can he compress invention out of pride,
Make heirship do the work of muscle, sail
Toward great discoveries with a pedigree?
Sick men ask cures, and Nature serves not hers
Daintily as a feast. A blacksmith once
Founded a dynasty, and raised on high
The leathern apron over armies spread
Between the mountains like a lake of steel. ·

FEDALMA (*bitterly*).

To be contemned, then, is fair augury.
That pledge of future good at least is ours

ZARCA.

Let men contemn us : 'tis such blind contempt
That leaves the wingéd broods to thrive in
    warmth
Unheeded, till they fill the air like storms
So we shall thrive—still darkly shall draw force
Into a new and multitudinous life
That likeness fashions to community,
Mother divine of customs, faith and laws.
'Tis ripeness, 'tis fame's zenith that kills hope.
Huge oaks are dying, forests yet to come
Lie in the twigs and rotten-seeming seeds.

FEDALMA.

And our wild Zíncali ?   'Neath their rough husk
Can you discern such seed?   You said our band
Was the best arm of some hard enterprise ;
They give out sparks of virtue, then, and show
There's metal in their earth ?

ZARCA.

Ay, metal fine
In my brave Gypsies.   Not the lithest Moor
Has lither limbs for scaling, keener eye
To mark the meaning of the furthest speck
That tells of change ; and they are disciplined
By faith in me, to such obedience
As needs no spy.   My scalers and my scouts
Are to the Moorish force they're leagued withal
As bow-string to the bow ; while I their chief
Command the enterprise and guide the will
Of Moorish captains, as the pilot guides
With eye-instructed hand the passive helm.
For high device is still the highest force,
And he who holds the secret of the wheel
May make the rivers do what work he would.
With thoughts impalpable we clutch men's souls,
Weaken the joints of armies, make them fly
Like dust and leaves before the viewless wind.
Tell me what's mirrored in the tiger's heart,
I'll rule that too.

FEDALMA (*wrought to a glow of admiration*).

O my imperial father !
'Tis where there breathes a mighty soul like yours
That men's contempt is of good augury.

ZARCA (*seizing both* FEDALMA'S *hands, and
looking at her searchingly*).

And you, my daughter, what are you—if not
The Zíncalo's child ?   Say, does not his great hope

Thrill in your veins like shouts of victory?
'Tis a vile life that like a garden pool
Lies stagnant in the round of personal loves ;
That has no ear save for the tickling lute
Set to small measures—deaf to all the beats
Of that large music rolling o'er the world :
A miserable, petty, low-roofed life,
That knows the mighty orbits of the skies
Through nought save light or dark in its own
      cabin.
The very brutes will feel the force of kind
And move together, gathering a new soul—
The soul of multitudes.   Say now, my child,
You will not falter, not look back and long
For unfledged ease in some soft alien nest.
The crane with outspread wing that heads the file
Pauses not, feels no backward impulses :
Behind it summer was, and is no more ;
Before it lies the summer it will reach
Or perish in mid-ocean.   You no less
Must feel the force sublime of growing life.
New thoughts are urgent as the growth of wings ;
The widening vision is imperious
As higher members bursting the worm's sheath.
You cannot grovel in the worm's delights :
You must take wingéd pleasures, wingéd pains.
Are you not steadfast?   Will you live or die
For aught below your royal heritage ?
To him who holds the flickering brief torch
That lights a beacon for the perishing,
Aught else is crime.   Would you let drop the
      torch ?

FEDALMA.

Father, my soul is weak, the mist of tears
Still rises to my eyes, and hides the goal
Which to your undimmed sight is fixed and clear.

But if I cannot plant resolve on hope,
It will stand firm on certainty of woe.
I choose the ill that is most like to end
With my poor being.   Hopes have precarious life.
They are oft blighted, withered, snapped sheer off
In vigorous growth and turned to rottenness.
But faithfulness can feed on suffering,
And knows no disappointment.   Trust in me !
If it were needed, this poor trembling hand
Should grasp the torch—strive not to let it fall
Though it were burning down close to my flesh,
No beacon lighted yet : through the damp dark
I should still hear the cry of gasping swimmers.
Father, I will be true !

ZARCA.

I trust that word.
And, for your sadness—you are young—the bruise
Will leave no mark.   The worst of misery
Is when a nature framed for noblest things
Condemns itself in youth to petty joys,
And, sore athirst for air, breathes scanty life
Gasping from out the shallows.   You are saved
From such poor doubleness.   The life we choose
Breathes high, and sees a full arched firmament.
Our deeds shall speak like rock-hewn messages,
Teaching great purpose to the distant time.
Now I must hasten back.   I shall but speak
To Nadar of the order he must keep
In setting watch and victualling.   The stars
And the young moon must see me at my post.
Nay, rest you here.   Farewell, my younger self—
Strong-hearted daughter ! Shall I live in you
When the earth covers me ?

FEDALMA.

My father, death
Should give your will divineness, make it strong

With the beseechings of a mighty soul
That left its work unfinished.   Kiss me now:

> (*They embrace, and she adds tremulously
> as they part,*)

And when you see fair hair, be pitiful.

[*Exit* ZARCA.

> (FEDALMA *seats herself on the bank, leans
> her head forward, and covers her face
> with her drapery.   While she is seated
> thus,* HINDA *comes from the bank, with
> a branch of musk roses in her hand.
> Seeing* FEDALMA *with head bent and
> covered, she pauses, and begins to move
> on tiptoe.*)

HINDA.

Our Queen !   Can she be crying ?   There she sits
As I did every day when my dog Saad
Sickened and yelled, and seemed to yell so loud
After we buried him, I oped his grave.

> (*She comes forward on tiptoe, kneels at* FE-
> DALMA'S *feet, and embraces them.*
> FEDALMA *uncovers her head.*)

FEDALMA.

Hinda ! what is it ?

HINDA.

Queen, a branch of roses—
So sweet, you'll love to smell them.   'Twas the
    last.
I climbed the bank to get it before Tralla,
And slipped and scratched my arm.   But I don't
    mind.
You love the roses—so do I.   I wish
The sky would rain down roses, as they rain

From off the shaken bush.   Why will it not ?
Then all the valley would be pink and white
And soft to tread on.   They would fall as light
As feathers, smelling sweet ; and it would be
Like sleeping and yet waking, all at once !
Over the sea, Queen, where we soon shall go,
Will it rain roses ?

FEDALMA.

No, my prattler, no !
It never will rain roses : when we want
To have more roses we must plant more trees.
But you want nothing, little one—the world
Just suits you as it suits the tawny squirrels.
Come, you want nothing.

HINDA.

Yes, I want more berries—
Red ones—to wind about my neck and arms
When I am married—on my ankles too
I want to wind red berries, and on my head.

FEDALMA.

Who is it you are fond of ?   Tell me, now.

HINDA.

O Queen, you know ! It could be no one else
But Ismaël.   He catches all the birds,
Knows where the speckled fish are, scales the
        rocks,
And sings and dances with me when I like.
How should I marry and not marry him ?

FEDALMA.

Should you have loved him, had he been a Moor,
Or white Castilian ?

HINDA (*starting to her feet, then kneeling again*).

Are you angry, Queen?
Say why you will think shame of your poor
      Hinda?
She'd sooner be a rat and hang on thorns
To parch until the wind had scattered her,
Than be an outcast, spit at by her tribe.

FEDALMA.

I think no evil—am not angry, child.
But would you part from Ismaël? leave him now
If your chief bade you—said it was for good
To all your tribe that you must part from him?

HINDA (*giving a sharp cry*).

Ah, will he say so?

FEDALMA (*almost fierce in her earnestness*).

Nay, child, answer me.
Could you leave Ismaël? get into a boat
And see the waters widen 'twixt you two
Till all was water and you saw him not,
And knew that you would never see him more?
If 'twas your chief's command, and if he said
Your tribe would all be slaughtered, die of plague,
Of famine—madly drink each other's blood . . .

HINDA (*trembling*).

O Queen, if it is so, tell Ismaël.

FEDALMA.

You would obey, then? part from him forever?

HINDA.

How could we live else? With our brethren
      lost?—
No marriage feast? The day would turn to dark.
A Zíncala cannot live without her tribe.

I must obey! Poor Ismaël—poor Hinda!
But will it ever be so cold and dark?
Oh, I would sit upon the rocks and cry,
And cry so long that I could cry no more :
Then I should go to sleep.

FEDALMA.

                         No, Hinda, no!
Thou never shalt be called to part from him.
I will have berries for thee, red and black,
And I will be so glad to see thee glad,
That earth will seem to hold enough of joy
To outweigh all the pangs of those who part.
Be comforted, bright eyes.   See, I will tie
These roses in a crown, for thee to wear.

HINDA (*clapping her hands, while* FEDALMA
        puts the roses on her head).

Oh, I'm as glad as many little foxes—
I will find Ismaël, and tell him all.
                         (*She runs off.*)

FEDALMA (*alone*).

She has the strength I lack.   Within her world
The dial has not stirred since first she woke :
No changing light has made the shadows die,
And taught her trusting soul sad difference.
For her, good, right, and law are all summed up
In what is possible : life is one web
Where love, joy, kindred, and obedience
Lie fast and even, in one warp and woof
With thirst and drinking, hunger, food, and
        sleep.
She knows no struggles, sees no double path :
Her fate is freedom, for her will is one
With her own people's law, the only law
She ever knew.   For me—I have fire within,
But on my will there falls the chilling snow

Of thoughts that come as subtly as soft flakes,
Yet press at last with hard and icy weight.
I could be firm, could give myself the wrench
And walk erect, hiding my life-long wound,
If I but saw the fruit of all my pain
With that strong vision which commands the
     soul,
And makes great awe the monarch of desire.
But now I totter, seeing no far goal :
I tread the rocky pass, and pause and grasp,
Guided by flashes.   When my father comes,
And breathes into my soul his generous hope—
By his own greatness making life seem great,
As the clear heavens bring sublimity,
And show earth larger, spanned by that blue
     vast—
Resolve is strong : I can embrace my sorrow,
Nor nicely weigh the fruit ; possessed with need
Solely to do the noblest, though it failed—
Though lava streamed upon my breathing deed
And buried it in night and barrenness.
But soon the glow dies out, the trumpet strain
That vibrated as strength through all my limbs
Is heard no longer ; over the wide scene
There's nought but chill gray silence, or the hum
And fitful discord of a vulgar world.
Then I sink helpless—sink into the arms
Of all sweet memories, and dream of bliss :
See looks that penetrate like tones ; hear tones
That flash looks with them.   Even now I feel
Soft airs enwrap me, as if yearning rays
Of some far presence touched me with their
     warmth
And brought a tender murmuring . . .

                  [While she mused,
A figure came from out the olive trees

That bent close-whispering 'twixt the parted hills
Beyond the crescent of thick cactus : paused
At sight of her ; then slowly forward moved
With careful steps, and gently said, " FEDALMA !"
Fearing lest fancy had enslaved her sense,
She quivered, rose, but turned not. Soon again :
" FEDALMA, it is SILVA !" Then she turned.
He, with bared head and arms entreating,
    beamed
Like morning on her. Vision held her still
One moment, then with gliding motion swift,
Inevitable as the melting stream's,
She found her rest within his circling arms.]

FEDALMA.

O love, you are living, and believe in me !

DON SILVA.

Once more we are together. Wishing dies—
Stifled with bliss.

FEDALMA.

          You did not hate me, then—
Think me an ingrate—think my love was small
That I forsook you ?

DON SILVA.

          Dear, I trusted you
As holy men trust God. You could do nought
That was not pure and loving—though the deed
Might pierce me unto death. You had less
    trust,
Since you suspected mine. 'Twas wicked doubt.

FEDALMA.

Nay, when I saw you hating me, the fault
Seemed in my lot—my bitter birthright—hers
On whom you lavished all your wealth of love

As price of nought but sorrow.   Then I said,
" 'Tis better so.   He will be happier !"
But soon that thought, struggling to be a hope,
Would end in tears.

DON SILVA.

It was a cruel thought.
Happier !   True misery is not begun
Until I cease to love thee.

FEDALMA.

Silva !

DON SILVA.

Mine !
(*They stand a moment or two in silence.*)

FEDALMA.

I thought I had so much to tell you, love—
Long eloquent stories—how it all befell—
The solemn message, calling me away
To awful spousals, where my own dead joy,
A conscious ghost, looked on and saw me wed.

DON SILVA.

Oh, that grave speech would cumber our quick
     souls
Like bells that waste the moments with their loud-
     ness.

FEDALMA.

And if it all were said, 'twould end in this,
That I still loved you when I fled away.
'Tis no more wisdom than the little birds
Make known by their soft twitter when they feel
Each other's heart beat.

DON SILVA.

　　　　　　　All the deepest things
We now say with our eyes and meeting pulse :
Our voices need but prattle.

FEDALMA.

　　　　　　　　　I forget
All the drear days of thirst in this one draught.

　　　(*Again they are silent for a few moments.*)

But tell me how you came? Where are your
　　　guards?
Is there no risk? And now I look at you,
This garb is strange . . .

DON SILVA.

　　　　　　　　I came alone.

FEDALMA.

　　　　　　　　　　Alone?

DON SILVA.

Yes—fled in secret. There was no way else
To find you safely.

FEDALMA (*letting one hand fall and moving a
little from him with a look of sudden terror,
while he clasps her more firmly by the other
arm*).
　　　　　　　Silva!

DON SILVA.

　　　　　　　　　It is nought.
Enough that I am here. Now we will cling.
What power shall hinder us? You left me once
To set your father free. That task is done,
And you are mine again. I have braved all
That I might find you, see your father, win
His furtherance in bearing you away
To some safe refuge. Are we not betrothed?

FEDALMA.

Oh, I am trembling 'neath the rush of thoughts
That come like griefs at morning—look at me
With awful faces, from the vanishing haze
That momently had hidden them.

DON SILVA.

What thoughts ?

FEDALMA.

Forgotten burials.   There lies a grave
Between this visionary present and the past.
Our joy is dead, and only smiles on us
A loving shade from out the place of tombs.

DON SILVA.

Your love is faint, else aught that parted us
Would seem but superstition.   Love supreme
Defies dream-terrors—risks avenging fires.
I have risked all things.   But your love is faint.

FEDALMA (*retreating a little, but keeping his
hand.*

Silva, if now between us came a sword,
Severed my arm, and left our two hands clasped,
This poor maimed arm would feel the clasp till
        death.
What parts us is a sword . . .

> (ZARCA *has been advancing in the back-
> ground.   He has drawn his sword,
> and now thrusts the naked blade be-
> tween them.* DON SILVA *lets go* FEDAL-
> MA'S *hand, and grasps his sword.*
> FEDALMA, *startled at first, stands
> firmly, as if prepared to interpose
> between her Father and the Duke.*)

ZARCA.

Ay, 'tis a sword
That parts the Spaniard and the Zíncala :
A sword that was baptized in Christian blood,
When once a band, cloaking with Spanish law
Their brutal rapine, would have butchered us,
And outraged then our women.

(*Resting the point of his sword on the ground.*)

My lord Duke,
I was a guest within your fortress once
Against my will ; had entertainment too—
Much like a galley-slave's.   Pray, have you
        sought
The Zíncalo's camp, to find a fit return
For that Castilian courtesy ? or rather
To make amends for all our prisoned toil
By free bestowal of your presence here ?

DON SILVA.

Chief, I have brought no scorn to meet your
        scorn.
I came because love urged me—that deep love
I bear to her whom you call daughter—her
Whom I reclaim as my betrothéd bride.

ZARCA.

Doubtless you bring for final argument
Your men-at-arms who will escort your bride ?

DON SILVA.

I came alone.   The only force I bring
Is tenderness.   Nay, I will trust besides
In all the pleadings of a father's care
To wed his daughter as her nurture bids.
And for your tribe—whatever purposed good
Your thoughts may cherish, I will make secure

With the strong surety of a noble's power :
My wealth shall be your treasury.

ZARCA (*with irony*).

                           My thanks !
To me you offer liberal price ; for her
Your love's beseeching will be force supreme.
She will go with you as a willing slave,
Will give a word of parting to her father,
Wave farewells to her tribe, then turn and say,
" Now, my lord, I am nothing but your bride ;
I am quite culled, have neither root nor trunk,
Now wear me with your plume !"

DON SILVA.

                        Yours is the wrong
Feigning in me one thought of her below
The highest homage.   I would make my rank
The pedestal of her worth ; a noble's sword,
A noble's honor, her defence ; his love
The life-long sanctuary of her womanhood.

ZARCA.

I tell you, were you King of Aragon,
And won my daughter's hand, your higher rank
Would blacken her dishonor.   'Twere excuse
If you were beggared, homeless, spit upon,
And so made even with her people's lot ;
For then she would be lured by want, not wealth,
To be a wife amongst an alien race
To whom her tribe owes curses.

DON SILVA.

                          Such blind hate
Is fit for beasts of prey, but not for men.
My hostile acts against you, should but count
As ignorant strokes against a friend unknown ;
And for the wrongs inflicted on your tribe

By Spanish edicts or the cruelty
Of Spanish vassals, am I criminal?
Love comes to cancel all ancestral hate,
Subdues all heritage, proves that in mankind
Union is deeper than division.

                    ZARCA.
                                   Ay,
Such love is common: I have seen it oft—
Seen many women rend the sacred ties
That bind them in high fellowship with men,
Making them mothers of a people's virtue:
Seen them so levelled to a handsome steed
That yesterday was Moorish property,
To-day is Christian—wears new-fashioned gear,
Neighs to new feeders, and will prance alike
Under all banners, so the banner be
A master's who caresses. Such light change
You call conversion; but we Zíncali call
Conversion infamy. Our people's faith
Is faithfulness; not the rote-learned belief
That we are heaven's highest favorites,
But the resolve that being most forsaken
Among the sons of men, we will be true
Each to the other, and our common lot.
You Christians burn men for their heresy:
Our vilest heretic is that Zíncala
Who, choosing ease, forsakes her people's woes.
The dowry of my daughter is to be
Chief woman of her tribe, and rescue it.
A bride with such a dowry has no match
Among the subjects of that Catholic Queen
Who would have Gypsies swept into the sea
Or else would have them gibbeted.

                    DON SILVA.
                              And you,
Fedalma's father—you who claim the dues

Of fatherhood—will offer up her youth
To mere grim idols of your phantasy!
Worse than all Pagans, with no oracle
To bid you murder, no sure good to win,
Will sacrifice your daughter—to no god,
But to a ravenous fire within your soul,
Mad hopes, blind hate, that like possessing fiends
Shriek at a name!   This sweetest virgin, reared
As garden flowers, to give the sordid world
Glimpses of perfectness, you snatch and thrust
On dreary wilds; in visions mad, proclaim
Semiramis of Gypsy wanderers;
Doom, with a broken arrow in her heart,
To wait for death 'mid squalid savages:
For what?   You would be saviour of your tribe;
So said Fedalma's letter; rather say,
You have the will to save by ruling men,
But first to rule; and with that flinty will
You cut your way, though the first cut you give
Gash your child's bosom.

> (*While* DON SILVA *has been speaking, with
> growing passion,* FEDALMA *has placed
> herself between him and her father.*)

ZARCA (*with calm irony*).

                    You are loud, my lord!
You only are the reasonable man;
You have a heart, I none.   Fedalma's good
Is what you see, you care for; while I seek
No good, not even my own, urged on by nought
But hellish hunger, which must still be fed,
Though in the feeding it I suffer throes.
Fume at your own opinion as you will:
I speak not now to you, but to my daughter.
If she still calls it good to mate with you,
To be a Spanish duchess, kneel at court,

And hope her beauty is excuse to men
When women whisper, "A mere Zincala!"
If she still calls it good to take a lot
That measures joy for her as she forgets
Her kindred and her kindred's misery,
Nor feels the softness of her downy couch
Marred by remembrance that she once forsook
The place that she was born to—let her go !
If life for her still lies in alien love,
That forces her to shut her soul from truth
As men in shameful pleasures shut out day ;
And death, for her, is to do rarest deeds,
Which, even failing, leave new faith to men,
The faith in human hearts—then, let her go !
She is my only offspring ; in her veins
She bears the blood her tribe has trusted in ;
Her heritage is their obedience,
And if I died, she might still lead them forth
To plant the race her lover now reviles
Where they may make a nation, and may rise
To grander manhood than his race can show ;
Then live a goddess, sanctifying oaths,
Enforcing right, and ruling consciences,
By law deep-graven in exalting deeds,
Through the long ages of her people's life.
If she can leave that lot for silken shame,
For kisses honeyed by oblivion—
The bliss of drunkards or the blank of fools—
Then let her go !   You Spanish Catholics,
When you are cruel, base, and treacherous,
For ends not pious, tender gifts to God,
And for men's wounds offer much oil to churches :
We have no altars for such healing gifts
As soothe the heavens for outrage done on earth.
We have no priesthood and no creed to teach
That she—the Zincala—who might save her race
And yet abandons it, may cleanse that blot,

And mend the curse her life has been to men,
By saving her own soul.   Her one base choice
Is wrong unchangeable, is poison shed
Where men must drink, shed by her poisoning
    will.
Now choose, Fedalma !

                    [But her choice was made.
Slowly, while yet her father spoke, she moved
From where oblique with deprecating arms
She stood between the two who swayed her heart :
Slowly she moved to choose sublimer pain ;
Yearning, yet shrinking ; wrought upon by awe,
Her own brief life seeming a little isle
Remote through visions of a wider world
With fates close-crowded ; firm to slay her joy
That cut her heart with smiles beneath the knife,
Like a sweet babe foredoomed by prophecy.
She stood apart, yet near her father : stood
Hand clutching hand, her limbs all tense with
    will
That strove 'gainst anguish, eyes that seemed a
    soul
Yearning in death toward him she loved and left.
He faced her, pale with passion and a will
Fierce to resist whatever might seem strong
And ask him to submit : he saw one end—
He must be conqueror ; monarch of his lot
And not its tributary.   But she spoke
Tenderly, pleadingly.]

        FEDALMA.

              My lord, farewell !
'Twas well we met once more ; now we must part.
I think we had the chief of all love's joys
Only in knowing that we loved each other.

DON SILVA.

I thought we loved with love that clings till
    death,
Clings as brute mothers bleeding to their young,
Still sheltering, clutching it, though it were dead ;
Taking the death-wound sooner than divide.
I thought we loved so.

FEDALMA.

        Silva, it is fate.
Great Fate has made me heiress of this woe.
You must forgive Fedalma all her debt :
She is quite beggared : if she gave herself,
'Twould be a self corrupt with stifled thoughts
Of a forsaken better.   It is truth
My father speaks : the Spanish noble's wife
Were a false Zincala.   No ! I will bear
The heavy trust of my inheritance.
See, 'twas my people's life that throbbed in me :
An unknown need stirred darkly in my soul,
And made me restless even in my bliss.
Oh, all my bliss was in our love ; but now
I may not taste it : some deep energy
Compels me to choose hunger.   Dear, farewell !
I must go with my people.

                [She stretched forth
Her tender hands, that oft had lain in his,
The hands he knew so well, that sight of them
Seemed like their touch.   But he stood still as
    death ;
Locked motionless by forces opposite :
His frustrate hopes still battled with despair ;
His will was prisoner to the double grasp
Of rage and hesitancy.   All the way
Behind him he had trodden confident,
Ruling munificently in his thought

This Gypsy father.   Now the father stood
Present and silent and unchangeable
As a celestial portent.   Backward lay
The traversed road, the town's forsaken wall,
The risk, the daring ; all around him now
Was obstacle, save where the rising flood
Of love close pressed by anguish of denial
Was sweeping him resistless ; save where she
Gazing stretched forth her tender hands, that hurt
Like parting kisses.   Then at last he spoke.]

DON SILVA.

No, I can never take those hands in mine
Then let them go forever !

FEDALMA.

                It must be.
We may not make this world a paradise
By walking it together hand in hand,
With eyes that meeting feed a double strength.
We must be only joined by pains divine
Of spirits blent in mutual memories.
Silva, our joy is dead.

DON SILVA.

              But love still lives,
And has a safer guard in wretchedness.
Fedalma, women know no perfect love :
Loving the strong, they can forsake the strong ;
Man clings because the being whom he loves
Is weak and needs him.   I can never turn
And leave you to your difficult wandering ;
Know that you tread the desert, bear the storm,
Shed tears, see terrors, faint with weariness,
Yet live away from you.   I should feel nought
But your imagined pains : in my own steps
See your feet bleeding, taste your silent tears,

And feel no presence but your loneliness.
No, I will never leave you !

ZARCA.

      My lord Duke,
I have been patient, given room for speech,
Bent not to move my daughter by command,
Save that of her own faithfulness. But now,
All further words are idle elegies
Unfitting times of action. You are here
With the safe-conduct of that trust you showed
Coming unguarded to the Gypsy's camp.
I would fain meet all trust with courtesy
As well as honor ; but my utmost power
Is to afford you Gypsy guard to-night
Within the tents that keep the northward lines,
And for the morrow, escort on your way
Back to the Moorish bounds.

DON SILVA.

      What if my words
Were meant for deeds, decisive as a leap
Into the current ? It is not my wont
To utter hollow words, and speak resolves
Like verses bandied in a madrigal.
I spoke in action first : I faced all risks
To find Fedalma. Action speaks again
When I, a Spanish noble, here declare
That I abide with her, adopt her lot,
Claiming alone the fulfilment of her vows
As my betrothéd wife.

FEDALMA (*wresting herself from him, and standing opposite with a look of terror*).

      Nay, Silva, nay !
You could not live so—spring from your high
  place . . .

Don Silva.

Yes, I have said it.   And you, chief, are bound
By her strict vows, no stronger fealty
Being left to cancel them.

Zarca.

        Strong words, my lord !
Sounds fatal as the hammer-strokes that shape
The glowing metal : they must shape your life.
That you will claim my daughter is to say
That you will leave your Spanish dignities,
Your home, your wealth, your people, to become
Wholly a Zíncalo : share our wanderings,
And be a match meet for my daughter's dower
By living for her tribe ; take the deep oath
That binds you to us ; rest within our camp,
Nevermore hold command of Spanish men,
And keep my orders.   See, my lord, you lock
A many-winding chain—a heavy chain.

Don Silva.

I have but one resolve : let the rest follow.
What is my rank ?   To-morrow it will be filled
By one who eyes it like a carrion bird,
Waiting for death.   I shall be no more missed
Than waves are missed that leaping on the rock
Find there a bed and rest.   Life's a vast sea
That does its mighty errand without fail,
Panting in unchanged strength though waves are
      changing.
And I have said it : she shall be my people,
And where she gives her life I will give mine.
She shall not live alone, nor die alone.
I will elect my deeds, and be the liege
Not of my birth, but of that good alone
I have discerned and chosen.

ZARCA.

                              Our poor faith
Allows not rightful choice, save of the right
Our birth has made for us.   And you, my lord,
Can still defer your choice, for some days' space.
I march perforce to-night ; you, if you will,
Under a Gypsy guard, can keep the heights
With silent Time that slowly opes the scroll
Of change inevitable—take no oath
Till my accomplished task leave me at large
To see you keep your purpose or renounce it.

DON SILVA.

Chief, do I hear amiss, or does your speech
Ring with a doubleness which I had held
Most alien to you?   You would put me off,
And cloak evasion with allowance ?   No !
We will complete our pledges.   I will take
That oath which binds not me alone, but you,
To join my life forever with Fedalma's.

ZARCA.

I wrangle not—time presses.   But the oath
Will leave you that same post upon the heights ;
Pledged to remain there while my absence lasts.
You are agreed, my lord ?

DON SILVA.
                    Agreed to all.

ZARCA.

Then I will give the summons to our camp.
We will adopt you as a brother now,
After our wonted fashion.
                              [*Exit* ZARCA.

(SILVA *takes* FEDALMA'S *hands*.)

FEDALMA.

       O my lord !
I think the earth is trembling : nought is firm.
Some terror chills me with a shadowy grasp.
Am I about to wake, or do you breathe
Here in this valley ? Did the outer air
Vibrate to fatal words, or did they shake
Only my dreaming soul ? You—join—our tribe ?

DON SILVA.

Is then your love too faint to raise belief
Up to that height ?

FEDALMA.

     Silva, had you but said
That you would die—that were an easy task
For you who oft have fronted death in war.
But so to live for me—you, used to rule—
You could not breathe the air my father breathes :
His presence is subjection. Go, my lord !
Fly, while there yet is time. Wait not to speak.
I will declare that I refused your love—
Would keep no vows to you . . .

DON SILVA.

       It is too late.
You shall not thrust me back to seek a good
Apart from you. And what good ? Why, to face
Your absence—all the want that drove me forth—
To work the will of a more tyrannous friend
Than any uncowled father. Life at least
Gives choice of ills ; forces me to defy,
But shall not force me to a weak defiance.
The power that threatened you, to master me,
That scorches like a cave-hid dragon's breath,
Sure of its victory in spite of hate,
Is what I last will bend to—most defy.
Your father has a chieftain's ends, befitting

A soldier's eye and arm : were he as strong
As the Moors' prophet, yet the prophet too
Had younger captains of illustrious fame
Among the infidels.   Let him command,
For when your father speaks, I shall hear you.
Life were no gain if you were lost to me :
I would straight go and seek the Moorish walls,
Challenge their bravest, and embrace swift death.
The Glorious Mother and her pitying Son
Are not Inquisitors, else their heaven were hell.
Perhaps they hate their cruel worshippers,
And let them feed on lies.   I'll rather trust
They love you and have sent me to defend you.

FEDALMA.

I made my creed so, just to suit my mood
And smooth all hardship, till my father came
And taught my soul by ruling it.   Since then
I cannot weave a dreaming happy creed
Where our love's happiness is not accursed.
My father shook my soul awake.   And you—
The bonds Fedalma may not break for you,
I cannot joy that you should break for her.

DON SILVA.

Oh, Spanish men are not a petty band
Where one deserter makes a fatal breach.
Men, even nobles, are more plenteous
Than steeds and armor ; and my weapons left
Will find new hands to wield them.   Arrogance
Makes itself champion of mankind, and holds
God's purpose maimed for one hidalgo lost.

See where your father comes and brings a crowd
Of witnesses to hear my oath of love ;
The low red sun glows on them like a fire.
This seems a valley in some strange new world,
Where we have found each other, my Fedalma.

BOOK IV.

Now twice the day had sunk from off the hills
While Silva kept his watch there, with the band
Of stalwart Gypsies.   When the sun was high
He slept ; then, waking, strained impatient eyes
To catch the promise of some moving form
That might be Juan—Juan who went and came
To soothe two hearts, and claimed nought for his
      own :
Friend more divine than all divinities,
Quenching his human thirst in others' joy.
All through the lingering nights and pale chill
      dawns
Juan had hovered near ; with delicate sense,
As of some breath from every changing mood,
Had spoken or kept silence ; touched his lute
To hint of melody, or poured brief strains
That seemed to make all sorrows natural,
Hardly worth weeping for, since life was short,
And shared by loving souls.   Such pity welled
Within the minstrel's heart of light-tongued Juan
For this doomed man, who with dream-shrouded
      eyes
Had stepped into a torrent as a brook,
Thinking to ford it and return at will,
And now waked helpless in the eddying flood,
Hemmed by its raging hurry.   Once that thought,
How easy wandering is, how hard and strict
The homeward way, had slipped from reverie
Into low-murmured song ;—(brief Spanish song
'Scaped him as sighs escape from other men).

Push off the boat,
  Quit, quit the shore,
    The stars will guide us back :—
O gathering cloud,
  O wide, wide sea,
    O waves that keep no track !

On through the pines !
  The pillared woods,
    Where silence breathes sweet breath :—
O labyrinth,
  O sunless gloom,
    The other side of death !

Such plaintive song had seemed to please the
    Duke—
Had seemed to melt all voices of reproach
To sympathetic sadness ; but his moods
Had grown more fitful with the growing hours,
And this soft murmur had the iterant voice
Of heartless Echo, whom no pain can move
To say aught else than we have said to her.
He spoke, impatient : "Juan, cease thy song.
Our whimpering poesy and small-paced tunes
Have no more utterance than the cricket's chirp
For souls that carry heaven and hell within."
Then Juan, lightly : "True, my lord, I chirp
For lack of soul ; some hungry poets chirp
For lack of bread. 'Twere wiser to sit down
And count the star-seed, till I fell asleep
With the cheap wine of pure stupidity."
And Silva, checked by courtesy : "Nay, Juan,
Were speech once good, the song were best of
    speech.
I meant, all life is but poor mockery :
Action, place, power, the visible wide world
Are tattered masquerading of this self,

This pulse of conscious mystery : all change,
Whether to high or low, is change of rags.
But for her love, I would not take a good
Save to burn out in battle, in a flame
Of madness that would feel no mangled limbs,
And die not knowing death, but passing straight
—Well, well, to other flames—in purgatory."
Keen Juan's ear caught the self-discontent
That vibrated beneath the changing tones
Of life-contemning scorn. Gently he said :
" But *with* her love, my lord, the world deserves
A higher rate ; were it but masquerade,
The rags were surely worth the wearing ?" " Yes.
No misery shall force me to repent
That I have loved her."

              So with wilful talk,
Fencing the wounded soul from beating winds
Of truth that came unasked, companionship
Made the hours lighter. And the Gypsy guard,
Trusting familiar Juan, were content,
At friendly hint from him, to still their songs
And busy jargon round the nightly fires.
Such sounds, the quick-conceiving poet knew
Would strike on Silva's agitated soul
Like mocking repetition of the oath
That bound him in strange clanship with the
      tribe
Of human panthers, flame-eyed, lithe-limbed,
      fierce,
Unrecking of time-woven subtleties
And high tribunals of a phantom-world.

But the third day, though Silva southward gazed
Till all the shadows slanted toward him, gazed
Till all the shadows died, no Juan came.
Now in his stead came loneliness, and Thought
Inexorable, fastening with firm chain

What is to what hath been.   Now awful Night,
The prime ancestral mystery, came down
Past all the generations of the stars,
And visited his soul with touch more close
Than when he kept that younger, briefer watch
Under the church's roof beside his arms,
And won his knighthood.
                              Well, this solitude,
This company with the enduring universe,
Whose mighty silence carrying all the past
Absorbs our history as with a breath,
Should give him more assurance, make him
          strong
In all contempt of that poor circumstance
Called human life—customs and bonds and laws
Wherewith men make a better or a worse,
Like children playing on a barren mound
Feigning a thing to strive for or avoid.
Thus Silva argued with his many-voiced self,
Whose thwarted needs, like angry multitudes,
Lured from the home that nurtured them to
          strength,
Made loud insurgence.   Thus he called on
          Thought,
On dexterous Thought, with its swift alchemy
To change all forms, dissolve all prejudice
Of man's long heritage, and yield him up
A crude fused world to fashion as he would.
Thought played him double ; seemed to wear the
          yoke
Of sovereign passion in the noon-day height
Of passion's prevalence ; but served anon
As tribune to the larger soul which brought
Loud-mingled cries from every human need
That ages had instructed into life.
He could not grasp Night's black blank mystery
And wear it for a spiritual garb

Creed-proof : he shuddered at its passionless
    touch.
On solitary souls, the universe
Looks down inhospitable ; the human heart
Finds nowhere shelter but in human kind.
He yearned toward images that had breath in
    them,
That sprang warm palpitant with memories
From streets and altars, from ancestral homes
Banners and trophies and the cherishing rays
Of shame and honor in the eyes of man.
These made the speech articulate of his soul,
That could not move to utterance of scorn
Save in words bred by fellowship ; could not feel
Resolve of hardest constancy to love
The firmer for the sorrows of the loved,
Save by concurrent energies high-wrought
To sensibilities transcending sense
Through close community, and long-shared pains
Of far-off generations.   All in vain
He sought the outlaw's strength, and made a
    right
Contemning that hereditary right
Which held dim habitations in his frame,
Mysterious haunts of echoes old and far,
The voice divine of human loyalty.
At home, among his people, he had played
In sceptic ease with saints and litanies,
And thunders of the Church that deadened fell
Through screens of priests plethoric.   Awe, un-
    scathed
By deeper trespass, slept without a dream.
But for such trespass as made outcasts, still
The ancient Furies lived with faces new
And lurked with lighter slumber than of old
O'er Catholic Spain, the land of sacred oaths
That might be broken.

Now the former life
Of close-linked fellowship, the life that made
His full-formed self, as the impregnate sap
Of years successive frames the full-branched
        tree—
Was present in one whole ; and that great trust
His deed had broken turned reproach on him
From faces of all witnesses who heard
His uttered pledges ; saw him hold high place
Centring reliance ; use rich privilege
That bound him like a victim-nourished god
By tacit covenant to shield and bless ;
Assume the Cross and take his knightly oath
Mature, deliberate : faces human all,
And some divine as well as human : His
Who hung supreme, the suffering Man divine
Above the altar ; Hers, the Mother pure
Whose glance informed his masculine tender-
        ness
With deepest reverence ; the Archangel armed,
Trampling man's enemy : all heroic forms
That fill the world of faith with voices, hearts,
And high companionship, to Silva now
Made but one inward and insistent world
With faces of his peers, with court and hall
And deference, and reverent vassalage,
And filial pieties—one current strong,
The warmly mingled life-blood of his mind,
Sustaining him even when he idly played
With rules, beliefs, charges, and ceremonies
As arbitrary fooling.   Such revenge
Is wrought by the long travail of mankind
On him who scorns it, and would shape his life
Without obedience.
                    But his warrior's pride
Would take no wounds save on the breast.   He
        faced

The fatal crowd : " I never shall repent !
If I have sinned, my sin was made for me
By men's perverseness.   There's no blameless life
Save for the passionless, no sanctities
But have the self-same roof and props with crime,
Or have their roots close interlaced with wrong.
If I had loved her less, been more a craven,
I had kept my place and won the easy praise
Of a true Spanish noble.   But I loved,
And, loving, dared—not Death the warrior
But Infamy that binds and strips, and holds
The brand and lash.   I have dared all for her.
She was my good—what other men call heaven,
And for the sake of it bear penances ;
Nay, some of old were baited, tortured, flayed
To win their heaven.   Heaven was their good,
She, mine.   And I have braved for her all fires
Certain or threatened ; for I go away
Beyond the reach of expiation—far away
From sacramental blessing.   Does God bless
No outlaw ?   Shut his absolution fast
In human breath ?   Is there no God for me
Save him whose cross I have forsaken ?—Well,
I am forever exiled—but with her !
She is dragged out into the wilderness ;
I, with my love, will be her providence.
I have a right to choose my good or ill,
A right to damn myself !   The ill is mine.
I never will repent !" . . .
Thus Silva, inwardly debating, all his ear
Turned into audience of a twofold mind ;
For even in tumult full-fraught consciousness
Had plenteous being for a self aloof
That gazed and listened, like a soul in dreams
Weaving the wondrous tale it marvels at.
But oft the conflict slackened, oft strong Love
With tidal energy returning laid

All other restlessness : Fedalma came,
And with her visionary presence brought
What seemed a waking in the warm spring morn.
He still was pacing on the stony earth
Under the deepening night ; the fresh-lit fires
Were flickering on dark forms and eyes that met
His forward and his backward tread ; but she,
She was within him, making his whole self
Mere correspondence with her image : sense,
In all its deep recesses where it keeps
The mystic stores of ecstasy, was turned
To memory that killed the hour, like wine.
Then Silva said, " She, by herself, is life.
What was my joy before I loved her—what
Shall heaven lure us with, love being lost ?"—
For he was young.
               But now around the fires
The Gypsy band felt freer ; Juan's song
Was no more there, nor Juan's friendly ways
For links of amity 'twixt their wild mood
And this strange brother, this pale Spanish duke,
Who with their Gypsy badge upon his breast
Took readier place within their alien hearts
As a marked captive, who would fain escape.
And Nadar, who commanded them, had known
The prison in Bedmár.   So now, in talk
Foreign to Spanish ears, they said their minds,
Discussed their chief's intent, the lot marked out
For this new brother.   Would he wed their
         queen ?
And some denied, saying their queen would wed
Only a Gypsy duke—one who would join
Their bands in Telemsán.   But others thought
Young Hassan was to wed her ; said their chief
Would never trust this noble of Castile,
Who in his very swearing was forsworn.
And then one fell to chanting, in wild notes

Recurrent like the moan of outshut winds,
The adjuration they were wont to use
To any Spaniard who would join their tribe :
Words of plain Spanish, lately stirred anew
And ready at new impulse.   Soon the rest,
Drawn to the stream of sound, made unison
Higher and lower, till the tidal sweep
Seemed to assail the Duke and close him round
With force dæmonic.   All debate till now
Had wrestled with the urgence of that oath
Already broken ; now the newer oath
Thrust its loud presence on him.   He stood still,
Close baited by loud-barking thoughts—fierce
        hounds
Of that Supreme, the irreversible Past.

The ZINCALI *sing.*

Brother, hear and take the curse,
    Curse of soul's and body's throes,
    If you hate not all our foes,
    Cling not fast to all our woes,
        Turn false Zíncalo !

May you be accurst
By hunger and by thirst
    By spikéd pangs,
    Starvation's fangs
Clutching you alone
When none but peering vultures hear your moan.
    Curst by burning hands,
        Curst by aching brow,
    When on sea-wide sands
        Fever lays you low ;
    By the maddened brain
When the running water glistens,
And the deaf ear listens, listens,

Prisoned fire within the vein,
On the tongue and on the lip
Not a sip
From the earth or skies;
Hot the desert lies
Pressed into your anguish,
Narrowing earth and narrowing sky
Into lonely misery.
Lonely may you languish
Through the day and through the night,
Hate the darkness, hate the light,
Pray and find no ear,
Feel no brother near,
Till on death you cry,
Death who passes by,
And anew you groan,
Scaring the vultures all to leave you living lone:
Curst by soul's and body's throes
If you love the dark men's foes,
Cling not fast to all the dark men's woes,
Turn false Zíncalo!
Swear to hate the cruel cross,
The silver cross!
Glittering, laughing at the blood
Shed below it in a flood
When it glitters over Moorish porches;
Laughing at the scent of flesh
When it glitters where the fagot scorches,
Burning life's mysterious mesh:
Blood of wandering Israël,
Blood of wandering Ismaël,
Blood, the drink of Christian scorn,
Blood of wanderers, sons of morn
Where the life of men began:
Swear to hate the cross!—
Sign of all the wanderers' foes,
Sign of all the wanderers' woes—

Else its curse light on you !
Else the curse upon you light
Of its sharp red-sworded might.
May it lie a blood-red blight
On all things within your sight :
On the white haze of the morn,
On the meadows and the corn,
On the sun and on the moon,
On the clearness of the noon,
On the darkness of the night.
May it fill your aching sight—
Red-cross sword and sword blood-red—
Till it press upon your head,
Till it lie within your brain,
Piercing sharp, a cross of pain,
Till it lie upon your heart,
   Burning hot, a cross of fire
Till from sense in every part
Pains have clustered like a stinging swarm
    In the cross's form,
And you see nought but the cross of blood,
And you feel nought but the cross of fire :
   Curst by all the cross's throes
   If you hate not all our foes,
   Cling not fast to all our woes,
    Turn false Zíncalo !

A fierce delight was in the Gypsies' chant :
They thought no more of Silva, only felt
Like those broad-chested rovers of the night
Who pour exuberant strength upon the air.
To him it seemed as if the hellish rhythm,
Revolving in long curves that slackened now,
Now hurried, sweeping round again to slackness,
Would cease no more.   What use to raise his
    voice,
Or grasp his weapon ?   He was powerless now,

With these new comrades of his future—he
Who had been wont to have his wishes feared
And guessed at as a hidden law for men.
Even the passive silence of the night
That left these howlers mastery, even the moon,
Rising and staring with a helpless face,
Angered him.   He was ready now to fly
At some loud throat, and give the signal so
For butchery of himself.
                              But suddenly
The sounds that travelled toward no foreseen close
Were torn right off and fringed into the night ;
Sharp Gypsy ears had caught the onward strain
Of kindred voices joining in the chant.
All started to their feet and mustered close,
Auguring long-waited summons.   It was come :
The summons to set forth and join their chief.
Fedalma had been called, and she was gone
Under safe escort, Juan following her :
The camp—the women, children, and old men—
Were moving slowly southward on the way
To Almería.   Silva learned no more.
He marched perforce ; what other goal was his
Than where Fedalma was?   And so he marched
Through the dim passes and o'er rising hills,
Not knowing whither, till the morning came.

*The Moorish hall in the castle at Bedmár. The
morning twilight dimly shows stains of blood
on the white marble floor; yet there has been
a careful restoration of order among the sparse
objects of furniture. Stretched on mats lie
three corpses, the faces bare, the bodies covered
with mantles. A little way off, with rolled
matting for a pillow, lies ZARCA, sleeping.
His chest and arms are bare; his weapons,
turban, mail-shirt, and other upper garments
lie on the floor beside him. In the outer gallery Zíncali are pacing, at intervals, past the
arched openings.*

ZARCA (*half rising and resting his elbow on the
pillow while he looks round*).

The morning ! I have slept for full three hours ;
Slept without dreams, save my daughter's face.
Its sadness waked me.   Soon she will be here,
Soon must outlive the worst of all the pains
Bred by false nurture in an alien home—
As if a lion in fangless infancy
Learned love of creatures that with fatal growth
It scents as natural prey, and grasps and tears,
Yet with heart-hunger yearns for, missing them.
She is a lioness.   And they—the race
That robbed me of her—reared her to this pain.
He will be crushed and torn. There was no help.
But she, my child, will bear it.   For strong
        souls
Live like fire-hearted suns to spend their strength
In farthest striving action ; breathe more free
In mighty anguish than in trivial ease.
Her sad face waked me.   I shall meet it soon
Waking . . .

   (*He rises and stands looking at the corpses.*)

As now I look on these pale dead,
These blossoming branches crushed beneath the
        fall
Of that broad trunk to which I laid my axe
With fullest foresight.   So will I ever face
In thought beforehand to its utmost reach
The consequences of my conscious deeds ;
So face them after, bring them to my bed,
And never drug my soul to sleep with lies.
If they are cruel, they shall be arraigned
By that true name ; they shall be justified
By my high purpose, by the clear-seen good
That grew into my vision as I grew,
And makes my nature's function, the full pulse
Of inbred kingship.   Catholics,
Arabs, and Hebrews, have their god apiece
To fight and conquer for them, or be bruised,
Like Allah now, yet keep avenging stores
Of patient wrath.   The Zíncali have no god
Who speaks to them and calls them his, unless
I, Zarca, carry living in my frame
The power divine that chooses them and saves.
" Life and more life unto the chosen, death
To all things living that would stifle them ! "
So speaks each god that makes a nation strong ;
Burns trees and brutes and slays all hindering
        men.
The Spaniards boast their god the strongest now ;
They win most towns by treachery, make most
        slaves,
Burn the most vines and men, and rob the most.
I fight against that strength, and in my turn
Slay these brave young who duteously strove.
Cruel? ay, it is cruel.   But, how else ?
To save, we kill ; each blow we strike at guilt
Hurts innocence with its shock.   Men might
        well seek

For purifying rites ; even pious deeds
Need washing.   But my cleansing waters flow
Solely from my intent.

> (*He turns away from the bodies to where
> his garments lie, but does not lift them.*)

                   And she must suffer !
But she has seen the unchangeable and bowed
Her head beneath the yoke.   And she will walk
No more in chilling twilight, for to-day
Rises our sun.   The difficult night is past ;
We keep the bridge no more, but cross it ; march
Forth to a land where all our wars shall be
With greedy obstinate plants that will not yield
Fruit for their nurture.   All our race shall come
From north, west, east, a kindred multitude,
And make large fellowship, and raise inspired
The shout divine, the unison of resolve.
So I, so she, will see our race redeemed.
And their keen love of family and tribe
Shall no more thrive on cunning, hide and lurk
In petty arts of abject hunted life,
But grow heroic in the sanctioning light,
And feed with ardent blood a nation's heart.
That is my work : and it is well begun.
On to achievement !

> (*He takes up the mail-shirt, and looks at
> then throws it down again.*)

                   No, I'll none of you !
To-day there'll be no fighting.   A few hours,
And I shall doff these garments of the Moor :
Till then I will walk lightly and breathe high.

SEPHARDO (*appearing at the archway leading into
the outer gallery*).

You bade me wake you . . .

ZARCA.

               Welcome, Doctor ; see,
With that small task I did but beckon you
To graver work.   You know these corpses ?

SEPHARDO.

                                      Yes.
I would they were not corpses.   Storms will lay
The fairest trees and leave the withered stumps.
This Alvar and the Duke were of one age,
And very loving friends.   I minded not
The sight of Don Diego's corpse, for death
Gave him some gentleness, and had he lived
I had still hated him.   But this young Alvar
Was doubly noble, as a gem that holds
Rare virtues in its lustre ; and his death
Will pierce Don Silva with a poisoned dart.
This fair and curly youth was Arias,
A son of the Pachecos ; this dark face . . .

ZARCA.

Enough ! you know their names.   I had divined
That they were near the Duke, most like had
        served
My daughter, were her friends ; so rescued them
From being flung upon the heap of slain.
Beseech you, Doctor, if you owe me aught
As having served your people, take the pains
To see these bodies buried decently.
And let their names be writ above their graves,
As those of brave young Spaniards who died well.
I needs must bear this womanhood in my heart—
Bearing my daughter there.   For once she
        prayed—
'Twas at our parting—" When you see fair hair
Be pitiful."   And I am forced to look

On fair heads living and be pitiless.
Your service, Doctor, will be done to her.

SEPHARDO.

A service doubly dear.   For these young dead,
And one less happy Spaniard who still lives,
Are offerings which I wrenched from out my
        heart,
Constrained by cries of Israel : while my hands
Rendered the victims at command, my eyes
Closed themselves vainly, as if vision lay
Through those poor loopholes only.   I will go
And see the graves dug by some cypresses.

ZARCA.

Meanwhile the bodies shall rest here.   Farewell.

(*Exit* SEPHARDO.)

Nay, 'tis no mockery.   She keeps me so
From hardening with the hardness of my acts.
This Spaniard shrouded in her love—I would
He lay here too that I might pity him.

Morning.—The Plaça Santiago in Bedmdr. A crowd of townsmen forming an outer circle : within, Zíncali and Moorish soldiers drawn up round the central space. On the higher ground in front of the church a stake with fagots heaped, and at a little distance a gibbet. Moorish music. ZARCA enters, wearing his gold necklace with the Gypsy badge of the flaming torch over the dress of a Moorish Captain, accompanied by a small band of armed Zíncali, who fall aside and range themselves with the other soldiers while he takes his stand in front of the stake and gibbet. The music ceases, and there is expectant silence.

ZARCA.

Men of Bedmár, well-wishers, and allies,
Whether of Moorish or of Hebrew blood,
Who, being galled by the hard Spaniard's yoke,
Have welcomed our quick conquest as release,
I, Zarca, chief of Spanish Gypsies, hold
By delegation of the Moorish King
Supreme command within this town and fort.
Nor will I, with false show of modesty,
Profess myself unworthy of this post,
For so I should but tax the giver's choice.
And, as ye know, while I was prisoner here,
Forging the bullets meant for Moorish hearts,
But likely now to reach another mark,
I learned the secrets of the town's defence,
Caught the loud whispers of your discontent,
And so could serve the purpose of the Moor
As the edge's keenness serves the weapon's weight.
My Zíncali, lynx-eyed and lithe of limb,
Tracked out the high Sierra's hidden path,
Guided the hard ascent, and were the first
To scale the walls and brave the showering stones.

In brief, I reached this rank through service done
By thought of mine and valor of my tribe,
Yet hold it but in trust, with readiness
To lay it down ; for we—the Zincali—
Will never pitch our tents again on land
The Spaniard grudges us : we seek a home
Where we may spread and ripen like the corn
By blessing of the sun and spacious earth.
Ye wish us well, I think, and are our friends?

CROWD.
Long life to Zarca and his Zincali !

ZARCA.
Now, for the cause of our assembling here.
'Twas my command that rescued from your hands
That Spanish Prior and Inquisitor
Whom in fierce retribution you had bound
And meant to burn, tied to a planted cross.
I rescued him with promise that his death
Should be more signal in its justice—made
Public in fullest sense, and orderly.
Here, then, you see the stake—slow death by fire ;
And there a gibbet—swift death by the cord.
Now hear me, Moors and Hebrews of Bedmár,
Our kindred by the warmth of Eastern blood !
Punishing cruel wrong by cruelty
We copy Christian crime.   Vengeance is just :
Justly we rid the earth of human fiends
Who carry hell for pattern in their souls.
But in high vengeance there is noble scorn :
It tortures not the torturer, nor gives
Iniquitous payment for iniquity.
The great avenging angel does not crawl
To kill the serpent with a mimic fang ;
IIe stands erect, with sword of keenest edge
That slays like lightning.   So too we will slay

The cruel man ; slay him because he works
Woe to mankind.   And I have given command
To pile these fagots, not to burn quick flesh,
But for a sign of that dire wrong to men
Which arms our wrath with justice.   While, to
    show
This Christian worshipper that we obey
A better law than his, he shall be led
Straight to the gibbet and to swiftest death.
For I, the chieftain of the Gypsies, will,
My people shed no blood but what is shed
In heat of battle or in judgment strict
With calm deliberation on the right.
Such is my will, and if it please you—well.

CROWD.

It pleases us.   Long life to Zarca !

ZARCA.

                         Hark !
The bell is striking, and they bring even own
The prisoner from the fort.   What, Nadar ?

NADAR (*has appeared, cutting the crowd, and ad-
    vancing toward* ZARCA *till he is near enough to
    speak in an undertone*).

                         Chief,
I have obeyed your word, have followed it
As water does the furrow in the rock.

ZARCA.

Your band is here ?

NADAR.

    Yes, and the Spaniard too.

ZARCA.

'Twas so I ordered.

NADAR.

          Ay, but this sleek hound,
Who slipped his collar off to join the wolves,
Has still a heart for none but kennelled brutes.
He rages at the taking of the town,
Says all his friends are butchered ; and one corpse
He stumbled on—well, I would sooner be
A murdered Gypsy's dog, and howl for him,
Than be this Spaniard.   Rage has made him
      whiter.
One townsman taunted him with his escape,
And thanked him for so favoring us. . . .

ZARCA.

                Enough.
You gave him my command that he should wait
Within the castle, till I saw him ?

NADAR.

             Yes.
But he defied me, broke away, ran loose
I know not whither ; he may soon be here.
I came to warn you, lest he work us harm.

ZARCA.

Fear not, I know the road I travel by :
Its turns are no surprises. He who rules
Must humor full as much as he commands ;
Must let men vow impossibilities ;
Grant folly's prayers that hinder folly's wish
And serve the ends of wisdom. Ah, he comes !

[Sweeping like some pale herald from the dead,
Whose shadow-nurtured eyes, dazed by full light,
See nought without, but give reverted sense
To the soul's imagery, Silva came,
The wondering people parting wide to get

Continuous sight of him as he passed on—
This high hidalgo, who through blooming years
Had shone on men with planetary calm,
Believed-in with all sacred images
And saints that must be taken as they were,
Though rendering meagre service for men's
     praise :
Bareheaded now, carrying an unsheathed sword,
And on his breast, where late he bore the cross,
Wearing the Gypsy badge ; his form aslant,
Driven, it seemed, by some invisible chase,
Right to the front of Zarca. There he paused.]

Don Silva.

Chief, you are treacherous, cruel, devilish !—
Relentless as a curse that once let loose
From lips of wrath, lives bodiless to destroy,
And darkly traps a man in nets of guilt
Which could not weave themselves in open day
Before his eyes. Oh, it was bitter wrong
To hold this knowledge locked within your mind,
To stand with waking eyes in broadest light,
And see me, dreaming, shed my kindred's blood.
'Tis horrible that men with hearts and hands
Should smile in silence like the firmament
And see a fellow-mortal draw a lot
On which themselves have written agony !
Such injury has no redress, no healing
Save what may lie in stemming further ill.
Poor balm for maiming ! Yet I come to claim it.

Zarca.

First prove your wrongs, and I will hear your
     claim.
Mind, you are not commander of Bedmár,
Nor duke, nor knight, nor anything for me,
Save a sworn Gypsy, subject with my tribe,

Over whose deeds my will is absolute.
You chose that lot, and would have railed at me
Had I refused it you : I warned you first
What oaths you had to take . . .

DON SILVA.

                        You never warned me
That you had linked yourself with Moorish men
To take this town and fortress of Bedmár—
Slay my near kinsman, him who held my place,
Our house's heir and guardian—slay my friend,
My chosen brother—desecrate the church
Where once my mother held me in her arms,
Making the holy chrism holier
With tears of joy that fell upon my brow !
You never warned . . .

ZARCA.

                        I warned you of your oath.
You shrank not, were resolved, were sure your
        place
Would never miss you, and you had your will.
I am no priest, and keep no consciences :
I keep my own place and my own command.

DON SILVA.

I said my place would never miss me—yes !
A thousand Spaniards died on that same day
And were not missed ; their garments clothed the
        backs
That else were bare. . . .

ZARCA.

                        But you were just the one
Above the thousand, had you known the die
That fate was throwing then.

Don Silva.

          You knew it—you !
With fiendish knowledge, smiling at the end.
You knew what snares had made my flying steps
Murderous ; you let me lock my soul with oaths
Which your acts made a hellish sacrament.
I say, you knew this as a fiend would know it,
And let me damn myself.

Zarca.

          The deed was done
Before you took your oath, or reached our camp,—
Done when you slipped in secret from the post
'Twas yours to keep, and not to meditate
If others might not fill it.   For your oath,
What man is he who brandishes a sword
In darkness, kills his friends, and rages then
Against the night that kept him ignorant ?
Should I, for one unstable Spaniard, quit
My steadfast ends as father and as chief ;
Renounce my daughter and my people's hope,
Lest a deserter should be made ashamed ?

Don Silva.

Your daughter—O great God ! I vent but mad-
    ness.
The past will never change.   I come to stem
Harm that may yet be hindered.   Chief—this
    stake—
Tell me who is to die ! Are you not bound
Yourself to him you took in fellowship ?
The town is yours ; let me but save the blood
That still is warm in men who were my . . .

Zarca.

          Peace !

They bring the prisoner.

[ZARCA waved his arm
With head averse, in peremptory sign
That 'twixt them now there should be space and
    silence.
Most eyes had turned to where the prisoner
Advanced among his guards ; and Silva too
Turned eagerly, all other striving quelled
By striving with the dread lest he should see
His thought outside him.   And he saw it there.
The prisoner was Father Isidor :
The man whom once he fiercely had accused
As author of his misdeeds—whose designs
Had forced him into fatal secrecy.
The imperious and inexorable Will
Was yoked, and he who had been pitiless
To Silva's love, was led to pitiless death.
O hateful victory of blind wishes—prayers
Which hell had overheard and swift fulfilled !
The triumph was a torture, turning all
The strength of passion into strength of pain.
Remorse was born within him, that dire birth
Which robs all else of nurture—cancerous,
Forcing each pulse to feed its anguish, turning
All sweetest residues of healthy life
To fibrous clutches of slow misery.
Silva had but rebelled—he was not free ;
And all the subtle cords that bound his soul
Were tightened by the strain of one rash leap
Made in defiance.   He accused no more,
But dumbly shrank before accusing throngs
Of thoughts, the impetuous recurrent rush
Of all his past-created, unchanged self.
The Father came bareheaded, frocked, a rope
Around his neck,—but clad with majesty,
The strength of resolute undivided souls
Who, owning law, obey it.   In his hand
He bore a crucifix, and praying, gazed

Solely on that white image.   But his guards
Parted in front, and paused as they approached
The centre where the stake was.   Isidor
Lifted his eyes to look around him—calm,
Prepared to speak last words of willingness
To meet his death—last words of faith unchanged,
That, working   for   Christ's   kingdom,   he   had
          wrought
Righteously.   But his glance met Silva's eyes
And drew him.   Even images of stone
Look living with reproach on him who maims,
Profanes, defiles them.   Silva penitent
Moved forward, would have knelt before the man
Who still was one with all the sacred things
That came back on him in their sacredness,
Kindred, and oaths, and awe, and mystery.
But at the sight, the Father thrust the cross
With deprecating act before him, and his face
Pale-quivering, flashed out horror like white light
Flashed from the angel's sword that dooming
          drave
The sinner to the wilderness.   He spoke.]

FATHER ISIDOR.

Back from me, traitorous and accursed man !
Defile not me, who grasp the holiest,
With touch or breath !   Thou foulest murderer !
Fouler than Cain who struck his brother down
In jealous rage, thou for thy base delight
Hast oped the gate for wolves to come and tear
Uncounted brethren, weak and strong alike,
The helpless priest, the warrior all unarmed
Against a faithless leader : on thy head
Will rest the sacrilege, on thy soul the blood.
These blind barbarians, misbelievers, Moors,
Are but as Pilate and his soldiery ;
Thou, Judas, weighted with that heaviest crime

Which deepens hell ! I warned you of this end.
A traitorous leader, false to God and man,
A knight apostate, you shall soon behold
Above your people's blood the light of flames
Kindled by you to burn me—burn the flesh
Twin with your father's. O most wretched man !
Whose memory shall be of broken oaths—
Broken for lust—I turn away mine eyes
Forever from you. See, the stake is ready
And I am ready too.

DON SILVA.

It shall not be !

*(Raising his sword, he rushes in front of
the guards who are advancing, and
impedes them.)*

If you are human, Chief, hear my demand !
Stretch not my soul upon the endless rack
Of this man's torture !

ZARCA.

Stand aside, my lord !
Put up your sword. You vowed obedience
To me, your chief. It was your latest vow.

DON SILVA.

No ! hew me from the spot, or fasten me
Amid the fagots too, if he must burn.

ZARCA.

What should befall that persecuting monk
Was fixed before you came : no cruelty,
No nicely measured torture, weight for weight
Of injury, no luscious-toothed revenge
That justifies the injurer by its joy :
I seek but rescue and security

For harmless men, and such security
Means death to vipers and inquisitors.
These fagots shall but innocently blaze
In sign of gladness, when this man is dead,
That one more torturer has left the earth.
'Tis not for infidels to burn live men
And ape the rules of Christian piety.
This hard oppressor shall not die by fire :
He mounts the gibbet, dies a speedy death,
That, like a transfixed dragon, he may cease
To vex mankind.   Quick, guards, and clear the
         path !

[As well-trained hounds that hold their fleetness
         tense
In watchful, loving fixity of dark eyes,
And move with movement of their master's will,
The Gypsies with a wavelike swiftness met
Around the Father, and in wheeling course
Passed beyond Silva to the gibbet's foot,
Behind their chieftain.   Sudden left alone
With weapon bare, the multitude aloof,
Silva was mazed in doubtful consciousness,
As one who slumbering in the day awakes
From striving into freedom, and yet feels
His sense half captive to intangible things ;
Then with a flush of new decision sheathed
His futile naked weapon, and strode quick
To Zarca, speaking with a voice new-toned,
The struggling soul's hoarse, suffocated cry
Beneath the grappling anguish of despair.]

DON SILVA.

You, Zincalo, devil, blackest infidel !
You cannot hate that man as you hate me !
Finish your torture—take me—lift me up
And let the crowd spit at me—every Moor

Shoot reeds at me, and kill me with slow death
Beneath the mid-day fervor of the sun—
Or crucify me with a thieving hound—
Slake your hate so, and I will thank it : spare me
Only this man !

ZARCA.

        Madman, I hate you not.
But if I did, my hate were poorly served
By my device, if I should strive to mix
A bitterer misery for you than to taste
With leisure of a soul in unharmed limbs
The flavor of your folly.   For my course,
It has a goal, and takes no truant path
Because of you.   I am your chief : to me
You're nought more than a Zíncalo in revolt.

DON SILVA.

No, I'm no Zíncalo !   I here disown
The name I took in madness.   Here I tear
This badge away.   I am a Catholic knight,
A Spaniard who will die a Spaniard's death !

[Hark ! while he casts the badge upon the ground
And tramples on it, Silva hears a shout :
Was it a shout that threatened him ?   He looked
From out the dizzying flames of his own rage
In hope of adversaries—and he saw above
The form of Father Isidor upswung
Convulsed with martyr throes ; and knew the
     shout
For wonted exultation of the crowd
When malefactors die—or saints, or heroes.
And now to him that white-frocked murdered
     form
Which hanging judged him as its murderer,

Turned to a symbol of his guilt, and stirred
Tremors till then unwaked. With sudden snatch
At something hidden in his breast, he strode
Right upon Zarca : at the instant, down
Fell the great Chief, and Silva, staggering back,
Heard not the Gypsies' shriek, felt not the fangs
Of their fierce grasp—heard, felt but Zarca's
    words
Which seemed his soul outleaping in a cry
And urging men to run like rival waves
Whose rivalry is but obedience.]

          ZARCA (*as he falls*).

My daughter ! call her ! Call my daughter !

NADAR (*supporting* ZARCA *and crying to the
      Gypsies who have clutched* SILVA).

                  Stay !
Tear not the Spaniard, tie him to the stake :
Hear what the Chief shall bid us—there is time !

[Swiftly they tied him, pleasing vengeance so
With promise that would leave them free to
    watch
Their stricken good, their Chief stretched help-
    lessly
Pillowed upon the strength of loving limbs.
He heaved low groans, but would not spend his
    breath
In useless words : he waited till *she* came,
Keeping his life within the citadel
Of one great hope. And now around him closed
(But in wide circle, checked by loving fear)
His people all, holding their wails suppressed
Lest Death believed-in should be over-bold :
All life hung on their Chief—he would not die ;

His image gone, there were no wholeness left
To make a world of for the Zíncali's thought.
Eager they stood, but hushed ; the outer crowd
Spoke only in low murmurs, and some climbed
And clung with legs and arms on perilous coigns,
Striving to see where that colossal life
Lay panting—lay a Titan struggling still
To hold and give the precious hidden fire
Before the stronger grappled him.   Above
The young bright morning cast athwart white
　　　walls
Her shadows blue, and with their clear-cut line,
Mildly relentless as the dial-hand's,
Measured the shrinking future of an hour
Which held a shrinking hope.   And all the while
The silent beat of time in each man's soul
Made aching pulses.
　　　　　　　But the cry, " She comes !"
Parted the crowd like waters : and she came.
Swiftly as once before, inspired with joy,
She flashed across the space and made new light,
Glowing upon the glow of evening,
So swiftly now she came, inspired with woe,
Strong with the strength of all her father's pain,
Thrilling her as with fire of rage divine
And battling energy.   She knew—saw all :
The stake with Silva bound—her father pierced—
To this she had been born : a second time
Her father called her to the task of life.

She knelt beside him.   Then he raised himself,
And on her face there flashed from his the light
As of a star that waned, but flames anew
In mighty dissolution : 'twas the flame
Of a surviving trust, in agony.
He spoke the parting prayer that was command,
Must sway her will, and reign invisibly.]

ZARCA.

My daughter, you have promised—you will live
To save our people. In my garments here
I carry written pledges from the Moor :
He will keep faith in Spain and Africa.
Your weakness may be stronger than my strength,
Winning more love. . . . I cannot tell **the**
   end. . . .
I held my people's good within my breast.
Behold, now I deliver it to you.
See, it still breathes unstrangled—if it dies,
Let not your failing will be murderer. . . .
Rise, tell our people now I wait in pain . . .
I cannot die until I hear them say
They will obey you.

     [Meek, she pressed her lips
With slow solemnity upon his brow,
Sealing her pledges.   Firmly then she rose,
And met her people's eyes with kindred gaze,
Dark-flashing, fired by effort strenuous
Trampling on pain.]

FEDALMA.

     Ye Zíncali all, who hear !
Your Chief is dying : I his daughter live
To do his dying will.   He asks you now
To promise me obedience as your Queen,
That we may seek the land he won for us,
And live the better life for which he toiled.
Speak now, and fill my father's dying ear
With promise that you will obey him dead,
Obeying me his child.

     [Straightway arose
A shout of promise, sharpening into cries
That seemed to plead despairingly with death.]

The Zincali.

We will obey !   Our Chief shall never die!
We will obey him—will obey our Queen!

[The shout unanimous, the concurrent rush
Of many voices, quiring shook the air
With multitudinous wave : now rose, now fell,
Then rose again, the echoes following slow,
As if the scattered brethren of the tribe
Had caught afar and joined the ready vow.
Then some could hold no longer, but must rush
To kiss his dying feet, and some to kiss
The hem of their Queen's garment.   But she
    raised
Her hand to hush them.   "Hark! your Chief
    may speak
Another wish."   Quickly she kneeled again,
While they upon the ground kept motionless,
With head outstretched.   They heard his words ;
    for now,
Grasping at Nadar's arm, he spoke more loud,
As one who, having fought and conquered, hurls
His strength away with hurling off his shield.]

Zarca.

Let loose the Spaniard ! give him back his sword ;
He cannot move to any vengeance more—
His soul is locked 'twixt two opposing crimes.
I charge you let him go unharmed and free
Now through your midst. . . .

                    [With that he sank again—
His breast heaved strongly tow'rd sharp sudden
    falls,
And all his life seemed needed for each breath :
Yet once he spoke.]

My daughter, lay your arm
Beneath my head . . . so . . . bend and breathe
    on me.
I cannot see you more . . . the Night is come.
Be strong . . . remember . . . I can only . . .
    die.

[His voice went into silence, but his breast
Heaved long and moaned: its broad strength
    kept a life
That heard nought, saw nought, save what once
    had been,
And what might be in days and realms afar—
Which now in pale procession faded on
Toward the thick darkness. And she bent
    above
In sacramental watch to see great Death,
Companion of her future, who would wear
Forever in her eyes her father's form.]

And yet she knew that hurrying feet had gone
To do the Chief's behest, and in her soul
He who was once its lord was being jarred
With loosening of cords, that would not loose
The tightening torture of his anguish. This—
Oh, she knew it !—knew it as martyrs knew
The prongs that tore their flesh, while yet their
    tongues
Refused the ease of lies. In moments high
Space widens in the soul. And so she knelt,
Clinging with piety and awed resolve
Beside this altar of her father's life,
Seeing long travel under solemn suns
Stretching beyond it ; never turned her eyes,
Yet felt that Silva passed ; beheld his face
Pale, vivid, all alone, imploring her
Across black waters fathomless.

                                And he passed.
The Gypsies made wide pathway, shrank aloof
As those who fear to touch the thing they hate,
Lest hate triumphant, mastering all the limbs,
Should tear, bite, crush, in spite of hindering will.
Slowly he walked, reluctant to be safe
And bear dishonored life which none assailed ;
Walked hesitatingly, all his frame instinct
With high-born spirit, never used to dread
Or crouch for smiles, yet stung, yet quivering
With helpless strength, and in his soul convulsed
By visions where pale horror held a lamp
Over wide-reaching crime.   Silence hung round :
It seemed the Plaça hushed itself to hear
His footsteps and the Chief's deep dying breath.
Eyes quickened in the stillness, and the light
Seemed one clear gaze upon his misery,
And yet he could not pass her without pause :
One instant he must pause and look at her ;
But with that glance at her averted head,
New-urged by pain he turned away and went,
Carrying forever with him what he fled—
Her murdered love—her love, a dear wronged
        ghost,
Facing him, beauteous, 'mid the throngs of hell.

O fallen and forsaken ! were no hearts
Amid that crowd, mindful of what had been ?—
Hearts such as wait on beggared royalty,
Or silent watch by sinners who despair ?

Silva had vanished.   That dismissed revenge
Made larger room for sorrow in fierce hearts ;
And sorrow filled them.   For the Chief was dead.
The mighty breast subsided slow to calm,
Slow from the face the ethereal spirit waned,
As wanes the parting glory from the heights,

And leaves them in their pallid majesty.
Fedalma kissed the marble lips, and said,
" He breathes no more."   And then a long loud
      wail,
Poured out upon the morning, made her light
Ghastly as smiles on some fair maniac's face
Smiling unconscious o'er her bridegroom's corse.
The wailing men in eager press closed round,
And made a shadowing pall beneath the sun.
They lifted reverent the prostrate strength,
Sceptred anew by death.   Fedalma walked
Tearless, erect, following the dead—her cries
Deep smothering in her breast, as one who guides
Her children through the wilds, and sees and
      knows
Of danger more than they, and feels more pangs,
Yet shrinks not, groans not, bearing in her heart
Their ignorant misery and their trust in her.

BOOK V.

THE eastward rocks of Almería's bay
Answer long farewells of the travelling sun
With softest glow as from an inward pulse
Changing and flushing: all the Moorish ships
Seem conscious too, and shoot out sudden
   shadows;
Their black hulls snatch a glory, and their sails
Show variegated radiance, gently stirred
Like broad wings poised. Two galleys moored
   apart
Show decks as busy as a home of ants
Storing new forage; from their sides the boats,
Slowly pushed off, anon with flashing oar
Make transit to the quay's smooth-quarried edge,
Where thronging Gypsies are in haste to lade
Each as it comes with grandames, babes, and
   wives,
Or with dust-tinted goods, the company
Of wandering years. Nought seems to lie un-
   moved,
For 'mid the throng the lights and shadows play,
And make all surface eager, while the boats
Sway restless as a horse that heard the shouts
And surging hum incessant. Naked limbs
With beauteous ease bend, lift, and throw, or raise
High signalling hands. The black-haired mother
   steps
Athwart the boat's edge, and with opened arms,
A wandering Isis outcast from the gods,

Leans toward her lifted little one.   The boat
Full-laden cuts the waves, and dirge-like cries
Rise and then fall within it as it moves
From high to lower and from bright to dark.
Hither and thither, grave white-turbaned Moors
Move helpfully, and some bring welcome gifts,
Bright stuffs and cutlery, and bags of seed
To make new waving crops in Africa.
Others aloof with folded arms slow-eyed
Survey man's labor, saying, " God is great ;"
Or seek with question deep the Gypsies' root,
And whether their false faith, being small, will
          prove
Less damning than the copious false creeds
Of Jews and Christians : Moslem subtlety
Found balanced reasons, warranting suspense
As to whose hell was deepest—'twas enough
That there was room for all.   Thus the sedate.
The younger heads were busy with the tale
Of that great Chief whose exploits helped the
          Moor.
And, talking still, they shouldered past their
          friends
Following some lure which held their distant gaze
To eastward of the quay, where yet remained
A low black tent close guarded all around
By well-armed Gypsies.   Fronting it above,
Raised by stone steps that sought a jutting strand,
Fedalma stood and marked with anxious watch
Each laden boat the remnant lessening
Of cargo on the shore, or traced the course
Of Nadar to and fro in hard command
Of noisy tumult ; imaging oft anew
How much of labor still deferred the hour
When they must lift the boat and bear away
Her father's coffin, and her feet must quit
This shore forever.   Motionless she stood,

Black-crowned with wreaths of many-shadowed
     hair ;
Black-robed, but bearing wide upon her breast
Her father's golden necklace and his badge.
Her limbs were motionless, but in her eyes
And in her breathing lip's soft tremulous curve
Was intense motion as of prisoned fire
Escaping subtly in outleaping thought.

She watches anxiously, and yet she dreams :
The busy moments now expand, now shrink
To narrowing swarms within the refluent space
Of changeful consciousness. For in her thought
Already she has left the fading shore,
Sails with her people, seeks an unknown land,
And bears the burning length of weary days
That parching fall upon her father's hope,
Which she must plant and see it wither only—
Wither and die. She saw the end begun.
The Gypsy hearts were not unfaithful : she
Was centre to the savage loyalty
Which vowed obedience to Zarca dead.
But soon their natures missed the constant stress
Of his command, that, while it fired, restrained
By urgency supreme, and left no play
To fickle impulse scattering desire.
They loved their Queen, trusted in Zarca's child,
Would bear her o'er the desert on their arms
And think the weight a gladsome victory ;
But that great force which knit them into one,
The invisible passion of her father's soul,
That wrought them visibly into its will,
And would have bound their lives with perma-
     nence,
Was gone. Already Hassan and two bands,
Drawn by fresh baits of gain, had newly sold
Their service to the Moors, despite her call,

Known as the echo of her father's will,
To all the tribe, that they should pass with her
Straightway to Telemsán.   They were not moved
By worse rebellion than the wilful wish
To fashion their own service ; they still meant
To come when it should suit them.   But she
    said,
This is the cloud no bigger than a hand,
Sure-threatening.   In a little while, the tribe
That was to be the ensign of the race,
And draw it into conscious union,
Itself would break in small and scattered bands
That, living on scant prey, would still disperse
And propagate forgetfulness.   Brief years,
And that great purpose fed with vital fire
That might have glowed for half a century,
Subduing, quickening, shaping, like a sun—
Would be a faint tradition, flickering low
In dying memories, fringing with dim light
The nearer dark.
             Far, far the future stretched
Beyond that busy present on the quay,
Far her straight path beyond it.   Yet she watched
To mark the growing hour, and yet in dream
Alternate she beheld another track,
And felt herself unseen pursuing it
Close to a wanderer, who with haggard gaze
Looked out on loneliness.   The backward years—
Oh, she would not forget them—would not drink
Of waters that brought rest, while he far off
Remembered.   " Father, I renounced the joy ;
You must forgive the sorrow."
             So she stood,
Her struggling life compressed into that hour,
Yearning, resolving, conquering ; though she
    seemed
Still as a tutelary image sent

To guard her people and to be the strength
Of some rock-citadel.

Below her sat
Slim mischievous Hinda, happy, red-bedecked
With rows of berries, grinning, nodding oft,
And shaking high her small dark arm and hand
Responsive to the black-maned Ismaël,
Who held aloft his spoil, and clad in skins
Seemed the Boy-prophet of the wilderness
Escaped from tasks prophetic. But anon
Hinda would backward turn upon her knees,
And like a pretty loving hound would bend
To fondle her Queen's feet, then lift her head
Hoping to feel the gently pressing palm
Which touched the deeper sense. Fedalma
        knew—
From out the black robe stretched her speaking
        hand
And shared the girl's content.

So the dire hours
Burthened with destiny—the death of hopes
Darkening long generations, or the birth
Of thoughts undying—such hours sweep along
In their aërial ocean measureless
Myriads of little joys, that ripen sweet
And soothe the sorrowful spirit of the world,
Groaning and travailing with the painful birth
Of slow redemption.

But emerging now
From eastward fringing lines of idling men
Quick Juan lightly sought the upward steps
Behind Fedalma, and two paces off,
With head uncovered, said in gentle tones,
" Lady Fedalma !"—(Juan's password now
Used by no other), and Fedalma turned,
Knowing who sought her. He advanced a
        step,

And meeting straight her large calm questioning
      gaze,
Warned her of some grave purport by a face
That told of trouble.   Lower still he spoke.

JUAN.

Look from me, lady, toward a moving form
That quits the crowd and seeks the lonelier
      strand—
A tall and gray-clad pilgrim. . . .

                        [Solemnly
His low tones fell on her, as if she passed
Into religious dimness among tombs,
And trod on names in everlasting rest.
Lingeringly she looked, and then with voice
Deep and yet soft, like notes from some long
      chord
Responsive to thrilled air, said—]

FEDALMA.

                 It is he !

[Juan kept silence for a little space,
With reverent caution, lest his lighter grief
Might seem a wanton touch upon her pain.
But time was urging him with visible flight,
Changing the shadows : he must utter all.]

JUAN.

That man was young when last I pressed his
      hand—
In that dread moment when he left Bedmár.
He has aged since : the week has made him gray.
And yet I knew him—knew the white-streaked
      hair
Before I saw his face, as I should know

The tear-dimmed writing of a friend.   See now—
Does he not linger—pause?——perhaps expect . .

[Juan pled timidly : Fedalma's eyes
Flashed ; and through all her frame there ran the
　　　shock
Of some sharp-wounding joy, like his who hastes
And dreads to come too late, and comes in time
To press a loved hand dying.   She was mute
And made no gesture : all her being paused
In resolution, as some leonine wave
That makes a moment's silence ere it leaps.]

JUAN.

He came from Carthagena, in a boat
Too slight for safety ; yon small two-oared boat
Below the rock ; the fisher-boy within
Awaits his signal.   But the pilgrim waits. . . .

FEDALMA.

Yes, I will go !—Father, I owe him this,
For loving me made all his misery.
And we will look once more—will say farewell
As in a solemn rite to strengthen us
For our eternal parting.   Juan, stay
Here in my place, to warn me, were there need
And, Hinda, follow me !

　　　　　　　　　[All men who watched
Lost her regretfully, then drew content
From thought that she must quickly come again,
And filled the time with striving to be near.

She, down the steps, along the sandy brink
To where he stood, walked firm ; with quickened
　　　step
The moment when each felt the other saw.

He moved at sight of her : their glances met ;
It seemed they could no more remain aloof
Than nearing waters hurrying into one.
Yet their steps slackened and they paused apart,
Pressed backward by the force of memories
Which reigned supreme as death above desire.
Two paces off they stood and silently
Looked at each other.   Was it well to speak ?
Could speech be clearer, stronger, tell them more
Than that long gaze of their renouncing love?
They passed from silence hardly knowing how ;
It seemed they heard each other's thought before.]

DON SILVA.

I go to be absolved, to have my life
Washed into fitness for an offering
To injured Spain.   But I have nought to give
For that last injury to her I loved
Better than I loved Spain.   I am accurst
Above all sinners, being made the curse
Of her I sinned for.   Pardon ?   Penitence ?
When they have done their utmost, still beyond
Out of their reach stands Injury unchanged
And changeless.   I should see it still in heaven—
Out of my reach, forever in my sight :
Wearing your grief, 'twould hide the smiling
        seraphs.
I bring no puling prayer, Fedalma—ask
No balm of pardon that may soothe my soul
For others' bleeding wounds : I am not come
To say, " Forgive me :" you must not forgive,
For you must see me ever as I am—
Your father's . . .

FEDALMA.

        Speak it not !   Calamity
Comes like a deluge and o'erfloods our crimes,

Till sin is hidden in woe. You—I—we two,
Grasping we knew not what, that seemed delight,
Opened the sluices of that deep.

DON SILVA.

We two ?—
Fedalma, you were blameless, helpless.

FEDALMA.

No !
It shall not be that you did aught alone.
For when we loved I willed to reign in you,
And I was jealous even of the day
If it could gladden you apart from me.
And so, it must be that I shared each deed
Our love was root of.

DON SILVA.

Dear ! you share the woe—
Nay, the worst dart of vengeance fell on you.

FEDALMA.

Vengeance ! She does but sweep us with her
        skirts—
She takes large space, and lies a baleful light
Revolving with long years—sees children's
        children,
Blights them in their prime. . . . Oh, if two
        lovers leaned
To breathe one air and spread a pestilence,
They would but lie two livid victims dead
Amid the city of the dying. We
With our poor petty lives have strangled one
That ages watch for vainly.

DON SILVA.

Deep despair
Fills all your tones as with slow agony.

Speak words that narrow anguish to some shape:
Tell me what dread is close before you ?

FEDALMA.

None.

No dread, but clear assurance of the end.
My father held within his mighty frame
A people's life : great futures died with him
Never to rise, until the time shall ripe
Some other hero with the will to save
The outcast Zincali.

DON SILVA.

And yet their shout—

I heard it—sounded as the plenteous rush
Of full-fed sources, shaking their wild souls
With power that promised sway.

FEDALMA.

Ah yes, that shout

Came from full hearts : they meant obedience.
But they are orphaned : their poor childish feet
Are vagabond in spite of love, and stray
Forgetful after little lures.   For me—
I am but as the funeral urn that bears
The ashes of a leader.

DON SILVA.

O great God !

What am I but a miserable brand
Lit by mysterious wrath ?   I lie cast down
A blackened branch upon the desolate ground
Where once I kindled ruin.   I shall drink
No cup of purest water but will taste
Bitter with thy lone hopelessness, Fedalma.

FEDALMA.

Nay, Silva, think of me as one who sees
A light serene and strong on one sole path
Which she will tread till death . . .
He trusted me, and I will keep his trust :
My life shall be its temple.   I will plant
His sacred hope within the sanctuary
And die its priestess—though I die alone,
A hoary woman on the altar-step,
Cold 'mid cold ashes.   That is my chief good.
The deepest hunger of a faithful heart
Is faithfulness.   Wish me nought else.   And
     you—
You too will live. . . .

DON SILVA.

            I go to Rome, to seek
The right to use my knightly sword again ;
The right to fill my place and live or die
So that all Spaniards shall not curse my name.
I sate one hour upon the barren rock
And longed to kill myself ; but then I said,
I will not leave my name in infamy,
I will not be perpetual rottenness
Upon the Spaniard's air.   If I must sink
At last to hell, I will not take my stand
Among the coward crew who could not bear
The harm themselves had done, which others
     bore.
My young life yet may fill some fatal breach,
And I will take no pardon, not my own,
Not God's—no pardon idly on my knees ;
But it shall come to me upon my feet
And in the thick of action, and each deed
That carried shame and wrong shall be the sting
That drives me higher up the steep of honor

In deeds of duteous service to that Spain
Who nourished me on her expectant breast,
The heir of highest gifts.   I will not fling
My earthly being down for carrion
To fill the air with loathing : I will be
The living prey of some fierce noble death
That leaps upon me while I move.   Aloud
I said, " I will redeem my name," and then—
I know not if aloud : I felt the words
Drinking up all my senses—" She still lives.
I would not quit the dear familiar earth
Where both of us behold the self-same sun,
Where there can be no strangeness 'twixt our
         thoughts
So deep as their communion."   Resolute
I rose and walked.—Fedalma, think of me
As one who will regain the only life
Where he is other than apostate—one
Who seeks but to renew and keep the vows
Of Spanish knight and noble.   But the breach
Outside those vows—the fatal second breach—
Lies a dark gulf where I have nought to cast,
Not even expiation—poor pretence,
Which changes nought but what survives the
         past,
And raises not the dead.   That deep dark gulf
Divides us.

FEDALMA.

                    Yes, forever.   We must walk
Apart unto the end.   Our marriage rite
Is our resolve that we will each be true
To high allegiance, higher than our love.
Our dear young love—its breath was happiness !
But it had grown upon a larger life
Which tore its roots asunder.   We rebelled—
The larger life subdued us.   Yet we are wed ;

For we shall carry each the pressure deep
Of the other's soul.   I soon shall leave the shore.
The winds to-night will bear me far away
My lord, farewell !

                  He did not say '' Farewell.''
But neither knew that he was silent.   She,
For one long moment, moved not.   They knew
      nought
Save that they parted ; for their mutual gaze
As with their soul's full speech forbade their
      hands
To seek each other—those oft-clasping hands
Which had a memory of their own, and went
Widowed of one dear touch for evermore.
At last she turned and with swift movement
      passed,
Beckoning to Hinda, who was bending low
And lingered still to wash her shells, but soon
Leaping and scampering followed, while her
      Queen
Mounted the steps again and took her place,
Which Juan rendered silently.
                     And now
The press upon the quay was thinned ; the
      ground
Was cleared of cumbering heaps, the eager shouts
Had sunk, and left a murmur more restrained
By common purpose.   All the men ashore
Were gathering into ordered companies,
And with less clamor filled the waiting boats,
As if the speaking light commanded them
To quiet speed : for now the farewell glow
Was on the topmost heights, and where far
      ships
Were southward tending, tranquil, slow, and
      white

Upon the luminous meadow toward the verge.
The quay was in still shadow, and the boats
Went sombrely upon the sombre waves.
Fedalma watched again ; but now her gaze
Takes in the eastward bay, where that small bark
Which held the fisher-boy floats weightier
With one more life, that rests upon the oar
Watching with her.   He would not go away
Till she was gone ; he would not turn his face
Away from her at parting : but the sea
Should widen slowly 'twixt their seeking eyes.

The time was coming.   Nadar had approached.
Was the Queen ready ?   Would she follow now
Her father's body ?   For the largest boat
Was waiting at the quay, the last strong band
Of Zíncali had ranged themselves in lines
To guard her passage and to follow her.
" Yes, I am ready ;" and with action prompt
They cast aside the Gypsy's wandering tomb,
And fenced the space from curious Moors who
          pressed
To see Chief Zarca's coffin as it lay.
They raised it slowly, holding it aloft
On shoulders proud to bear the heavy load.
Bound on the coffin lay the chieftain's arms,
His Gypsy garments and his coat of mail.
Fedalma saw the burthen lifted high,
And then descending followed.   All was still.
The Moors aloof could hear the struggling steps
Beneath the lowered burthen at the boat—
The struggling calls subdued, till safe released
It lay within, the space around it filled
By black-haired Gypsies.   Then Fedalma stepped
From off the shore and saw it flee away—
The land that bred her helping the resolve
Which exiled her forever.

It was night
Before the ships weighed anchor and gave sail:
Fresh Night emergent in her clearness, lit
By the large crescent moon, with Hesperus,
And those great stars that lead the eager host.
Fedalma stood and watched the little bark
Lying jet-black upon moon-whitened waves.
Silva was standing too.   He too divined
A steadfast form that held him with its thought,
And eyes that sought him vanishing : he saw
The waters widen slowly, till at last
Straining he gazed, and knew not if he gazed
On aught but blackness overhung by stars.

NOTES.

P. 41. *Cactus.*

THE Indian fig (*Opuntia*), like the other *Cactaceæ*, is believed to have been introduced into Europe from South America; but every one who has been in the south of Spain will understand why the anachronism has been chosen.

P. 142. *Marranos.*

The name given by the Spanish Jews to the multitudes of their race converted to Christianity at the end of the fourteenth century and beginning of the fifteenth. The lofty derivation from *Maran-atha*, the Lord cometh, seems hardly called for, seeing that *marrano* is Spanish for *pig*. The "old Christians" learned to use the word as a term of contempt for the "new Christians," or converted Jews and their descendants; but not too monotonously, for they often interchanged it with the fine old crusted opprobrium of the name *Jew*. Still, many Marranos held the highest secular and ecclesiastical prizes in Spain, and were respected accordingly.

P. 159. *Celestial Baron.*

The Spaniards conceived their patron Santiago (St. James), the great captain of their armies, as a knight and baron: to them, the incongruity would have lain in conceiving him simply as a Galilean fisherman. And their legend was adopted with respect by devout mediæval minds generally. Dante, in an elevated passage of the *Paradiso*—the memorable opening of *Canto* xxv. —chooses to introduce the Apostle James as *il barone*.

> " Indi si mosse un lume verso noi
> Di quella schiera, ond 'uscì la primizia
> Che lasciò Cristo de' vicari suoi.
> E la mia Donna piena de letizia
> Mi disse : Mira, mira, ecco 'l barone
> Per cui laggiù si visita Galizia."

P. 161.   *The Seven Parts.*

Las Siete Partidas (The Seven Parts) is the title given to the code of laws compiled under Alfonso the Tenth, who reigned in the latter half of the thirteenth century—1252-1284. The passage in the text is translated from *Partida II., Ley II.* The whole preamble is worth citing in its old Spanish :—

" *Como deben ser escogidos los caballeros.*"

" Antiguamiente para facer caballeros escogien de los venadores de monte, que son homes que sufren grande laceria, et carpinteros, et ferreros, et pedreros, porque usan mucho a ferir et son fuerte de manos ; et otrosi de los carniceros, por razon que usan matar las cosas vivas et esparcer la sangre dellas : et aun cataban otra cosa en escogiendolos que fuesen bien faccionadas de membros para ser recios, et fuertes et ligeros. Et esta manera de escoger usaron los antiguos muy grant tiempo ; mas porque despues vieron muchas vegadas que estos atales non habiendo vergüenza olvidaban todas estas cosas sobredichas, et en logar de vincer sus enemigos venciense ellos, tovieron por bien los sabidores destas cosas que catasen homes para esto que hobiesen natural-miente en sí vergüenza.   Et sobresto dixo un sabio que habie nombre VEGECIO que fabló de la órden de caballería, que la vergüenza vieda al caballero que non fuya de la batalla, et por ende ella le face ser vencedor ; ca mucho tovieron que era mejor el homo flaco et sofridor, que el fuerte et ligero para foir.   Et por esto sobre todas las otras cosas cataron que fuesen homes porque se guardasen de facer cosa por que podiesen caer en vergüenza : et porque estos fueron escogidos de buenos logares et algo, que quiere tanto decir en lenguage de España como bien, por eso los lla-maron fijosdalgo, que muestra atanto como fijos de bien.   Et en algunos otros logares los llamaron gentiles, et tomaron este nombre de gentileza que muestra atanto como nobleza de bondat, porque los gentiles fueron nobles homes et buenos, et vevieron mas ordenadamente que las otras gentes. Et esta gentileza aviene en tres maneras ; la una por linage, la segunda por saber, et la tercera por bondat de armas et de costumbres et de maneras. Et comoquier que estos que la ganan por su sabidoría ó por su bondat, son con derecho llamados nobles et gentiles, mayormiente lo son aquellos que la han por linage antiguamiente, et facen buena vida porque les viene de lueñe como por heredat : et por ende son mas encargados de facer bien et guardarse de yerro et de malestanza ; ca non tan solamiente quando lo facen resciben daño et vergüenza ellos mismos, ma aun aquellos onde ellos vienen."

THE END.

CPSIA information can be obtained at www.ICGtesting.com
Printed in the USA
BVOW08s1027201114

375990BV00025B/438/P